HIGHER EDUCATION RESEARCH METHODOLOGY

This book is for anyone who wishes to improve university teaching and learning through systematic inquiry. It provides advice, but also a constructive critique of research methods and, in turn, the authors also make a contribution to the theories of research methodology.

Topics covered include ontology, epistemology and engagement with academic literature, as well as research design approaches and methods of data collection. There is a keen focus on quality in both the analysis and evaluation of research and new models are proposed to help the new researcher. The authors conclude by examining the challenges in getting work published and close with some words on quality of thought and action.

The ideas in the book come from the authors' extensive experience in teaching research methods courses in higher education, health and the corporate sector, as well as several empirical research projects that have helped provide a methodology for higher education. It will be of particular interest to postgraduate students, academic developers and experienced academics from a wide variety of disciplines.

Ben Kei Daniel is Associate Professor in Higher Education at the University of Otago, New Zealand, where he teaches research methodology (quantitative, qualitative, and mixed methods) and educational technology. He is the convenor for educational technology for the university.

Tony Harland is Professor of Higher Education at the University of Otago, New Zealand. His main research interest is in the purposes of a university education. Tony teaches qualitative research methods and other topics such as learning theory, leadership and peer review.

HIGHER EDUCATION RESEARCH METHODOLOGY

A Step-by-Step Guide to the Research Process

Ben Kei Daniel and Tony Harland

Routledge
Taylor & Francis Group
LONDON AND NEW YORK

First published 2018
by Routledge
2 Park Square, Milton Park, Abingdon, Oxon OX14 4RN

and by Routledge
711 Third Avenue, New York, NY 10017

Routledge is an imprint of the Taylor & Francis Group, an informa business

© 2018 Ben Kei Daniel & Tony Harland

The right of Ben Kei Daniel & Tony Harland to be identified as authors of this work has been asserted by them in accordance with sections 77 and 78 of the Copyright, Designs and Patents Act 1988.

All rights reserved. No part of this book may be reprinted or reproduced or utilised in any form or by any electronic, mechanical, or other means, now known or hereafter invented, including photocopying and recording, or in any information storage or retrieval system, without permission in writing from the publishers.

Trademark notice: Product or corporate names may be trademarks or registered trademarks, and are used only for identification and explanation without intent to infringe.

British Library Cataloguing in Publication Data
A catalogue record for this book is available from the British Library

Library of Congress Cataloging in Publication Data
A catalog record for this book has been requested

ISBN: 978-1-138-55598-3 (hbk)
ISBN: 978-1-138-55600-3 (pbk)
ISBN: 978-1-315-14978-3 (ebk)

Typeset in Bembo
by Out of House Publishing

CONTENTS

Acknowledgements	*ix*
Foreword	*x*
Figures	*xii*
Tables	*xiii*

	Introduction	1
	1 The origin of the thesis	2
	2 What is research in higher education?	3
	3 Data sources	5
	Bibliography	10
1	The study of higher education	11
	Introduction	11
	1 The higher education community	12
	2 Research as a form of teaching	13
	3 The evolution of teaching research	15
	4 The intellectual exercise of qualitative research	16
	5 Discovery	16
	6 Jargon or disciplinary language?	17
	7 Research methodology as a field of inquiry in higher education	17
	Bibliography	18
2	Ontology and epistemology	19
	Introduction	19
	1 Ontology and epistemology	21

	2	*How ontology and epistemology are made explicit*	27
	3	*How research teams work and negotiate different philosophical positions*	30
	4	*Epistemic access*	32
		Conclusion	33
		Bibliography	36
3	Qualitative research approaches		37
	Introduction		37
	1	*Phenomenology*	38
	2	*Grounded theory*	40
	3	*Ethnography*	40
	4	*Narrative inquiry*	40
	5	*Case study*	42
		Conclusion	42
		Bibliography	43
4	Surveys and other quantitative approaches		44
	Introduction		44
	1	*Survey approaches*	46
	2	*Experimental approaches*	51
	3	*Statistical decision making*	53
		Conclusion	53
		Bibliography	55
5	Research methods		56
	Introduction		56
	1	*Interviews*	56
	2	*Focus groups*	60
	3	*Questionnaires*	61
	4	*Observational methods*	63
	5	*Video and interpersonal process recall (IPR)*	65
		Conclusion	67
		Bibliography	67
6	The single case		68
	Introduction		68
	1	*What is the potential of case study?*	70
	2	*Which forms of data are acceptable?*	71
	3	*When does analysis stop?*	72
	4	*What makes a quality case study?*	73

	Conclusion	75
	Bibliography	76
7	**Research tools**	78
	Introduction	78
	1 Tools for the qualitative researcher	79
	2 A multi-tool	80
	3 Discipline	82
	4 Reflections as a source of data	83
	Conclusion	84
	Bibliography	84
8	**Engaging with the literature**	85
	Introduction	85
	1 Developing a conceptual framework	87
	2 How to engage systematically with the literature	88
	3 Tools for reviewing the literature	90
	4 A non-systematic approach	94
	Conclusion	94
	Bibliography	97
9	**Qualitative data analysis**	98
	Introduction	98
	1 Data analysis process	99
	2 Coding qualitative data	100
	3 Intercoder reliability	103
	4 Theoretical approaches to data analysis	105
	Conclusion	107
	Bibliography	108
10	**Evaluating qualitative research**	111
	Introduction	111
	1 Trustworthiness	113
	2 Auditability	115
	3 Credibility	116
	4 Transferability	117
	Conclusion	117
	Bibliography	119
11	**Writing for publication**	122
	Introduction	122
	1 Mind the gap	123

    2 *A systematic inquiry made public*   124
    3 *The problems with submitted work*   125
    Conclusion   127
    Bibliography   128

12 Final words   129

Further reading   *132*
Index   *135*

ACKNOWLEDGEMENTS

This book could not have been written without all the postgraduate students who have studied with us, and our colleagues from other disciplines who have ventured into the higher education field. All these collaborations have enriched our experiences, forced us to think more critically about higher education methodologies and, most importantly, made our work much more pleasurable. Special thanks go to our outstanding colleagues in the Higher Education Development Centre at the University of Otago for sharing expertise, and for their kindness and friendship. We would also like to thank Andrew Barlow and all those who helped test and develop the Tripartite Model, and those who provided other sources of empirical data. After reading the foreword written by Dr Navé Wald, we finally understood what we had been trying to achieve with this book. So thank you, Navé, for framing the text and for your support. Most of all, we are eternally grateful to our partners, Michelle and Sarah, who have truly had to put up with so much over the years, but whose support and encouragement have been unwavering.

FOREWORD

At times rather explicitly, and occasionally more implicitly, this book addresses a number of *worthwhile* issues in the study of higher education. It contains plenty of practical advice that is both theoretically informed and based on the vast experience of the authors, who are teachers of higher education research, research supervisors and active researchers in the field, as well as peer reviewers for a number of leading journals. The credentials of the authors alone could be a sufficient justification for reading the book as a 'beginner's guide to research in higher education'; but that would simply undermine what this book truly seeks to achieve: a culture of quality critical inquiry in the field of higher education.

The authors may address issues of interest to prospective or emerging researchers, but the book's application is much wider than that. The careful use of 'worthwhile' as a rather hidden keyword is vital for understanding the book's wider importance to the field. When the authors note that 'any research of quality must have something worthwhile to say' (p. 2) and thus urge the reader to '[a]sk a worthwhile [research] question' (p. 17), they do not merely state the obvious or provide simple advice for novices. Instead, they offer a constructive but critical reflection on the field, and this is a timely and welcome contribution that should receive notice from emerging as well as established researchers. Put differently, research in higher education is too often largely descriptive, not sufficiently critical and rarely makes a theoretical contribution. The view that research into teaching and pedagogy ought to be practice-oriented does not justify a lack of criticality. Research methodology – the main subject of this book – is thus a good place from which change can emerge.

The book, therefore, should be read for the valuable practical advice it contains, but the reader must remain cognizant that ultimately a better understanding of ontology and epistemology (Chapter 2) and how to engage with the literature (Chapter 8) is about a collective effort to raise the quality of research into higher education. In a sense, this is both an insightful textbook and a manifesto for higher education research. Achieving that is no small feat given the unusual characteristics of the field. As an academic field, higher education is not so much interdisciplinary in the usual sense, but rather *supradisciplinary*. This means that academics from across the wide spectrum of academic disciplines may wish to develop an interest in the field, which equally belongs to everyone. This peculiarity makes research in higher education a diverse but contested terrain, which, as such, is susceptible to influences from different scholarly traditions. It is this unstable terrain that the authors address through the foundational common ground that is research methodology.

I make these comments not as an established expert in the academic field of higher education. Until quite recently, I could have been taken to belong to one of the two main groups this book was written for, that of academics from other fields who transition into higher education research. My transition was from human geography, a discipline that shares some commonalities with that of higher education as well as demonstrating differences. Both fields are in the social sciences and, as such, have experienced the so-called 'cultural turn' (an epistemological shift away from positivism and towards interpretivism, in which culture is seen as giving social life meaning and significance). However, this turn was neither complete nor spatially even. Even today, ontological and epistemological differences – mostly manifested by preferences for either quantitative or qualitative methodologies – are evident in both fields, and in the Anglo-American world there is a notable split between the US inclinations towards quantitative approaches vis-à-vis other English-speaking countries where qualitative approaches are more commonplace. Notwithstanding this similarity, as a new researcher in higher education, I wanted to know something about the unspoken politics of publishing in this field. Differences were quick to emerge. For example, many qualitative studies were still written in a 'science' format, to include methodology, results and discussion sections. Moreover, the literature component in many articles was fairly descriptive and not particularly critical. Debates and disagreements between scholars were difficult to find; perhaps because of a tendency to use overly polite language. Yet regardless of my personal preferences, values or beliefs regarding academic research and its purpose, this book provides numerous insights into these unspoken politics of doing and publishing research in higher education (see in particular Chapter 11).

It is not an easy task to provide relevant advice to both novice researchers and established researchers from other disciplines, but this book proves that it is possible. I will go even further to suggest that it has utility for more established academics in the higher education field and especially those who supervise postgraduate students. If the word wasn't imbued with too Marxist a connotation (that might drive away some readers), the book's title could have included the word 'manifesto'. Nevertheless, this is not an ordinary research methodology book and it should not be read as such.

Navé Wald

FIGURES

2.1	The building blocks of research (after Grix, 2002)	23
2.2	Ontological and epistemological features of methodology	26
2.3	The three main traditions of research and their relationship	27
4.1	Categories of sampling techniques	48
4.2	Decision diagram for choosing a statistical test	54
5.1	Interview context framework	59
5.2	Protocol for interpersonal process recall (IPR)	66
7.1	Reflections on the science field notebook	80
8.1	Steps in developing a conceptual framework	87
8.2	Framing a research area for review	88
8.3	The review process	89
8.4	The tripartite model	91
8.5	Hunting for knowledge	95
9.1	The process of undertaking qualitative research	99
9.2	The second stage of qualitative data analysis	101
9.3	The coding scheme and unit of analysis	102
9.4	Triple-coding qualitative analysis	103
9.5	Thematic analysis of qualitative data	106
10.1	Dimensions of the TACT framework	114
10.2	Testing the TACT framework	118
11.1	Forms of systematic inquiry	125

TABLES

1.1	People who study higher education	12
2.1	Five research paradigms with foundational knowledge values	25
2.2	Research types published in two major higher education journals	28
3.1	Conventional research approaches in higher education	39
4.1	Measurement scale and interpretation	45
5.1	Three types of interviews commonly used in higher education research	58
5.2	Types of questions in questionnaires	62
5.3	Summary of key points for questionnaire design	64
5.4	Types of observational method	64
6.1	Number of case studies published in four higher education journals, 2007–2012	69
6.2	Four challenges for learning case study in higher education	75
7.1	Categories of field note entries for observational studies (after McKernan, 1991)	81
8.1	Within-study analysis	92
8.2	Synthesis of the articles reviewed	94
9.1	Threshold per cent agreement levels	104
11.1	Why 161 articles were rejected after submission to a higher education journal	126

INTRODUCTION

This book is written primarily for university academics and postgraduate students who are new to the study of higher education. Readers will most likely be working in or studying higher education and so will be aiming to conduct research into their own practices, the places in which they work and the social and cultural phenomena related to higher education more generally. Collectively, these interdisciplinary inquiries make up the subject and field of higher education. A few researchers will have higher education as their first and only subject area. Many more will be researchers in other disciplines with an additional or secondary interest into an aspect of academic work relating to that discipline. These academics often research into teaching and learning challenges and new developments, but not exclusively so. Accordingly, the wider research community has a core of practitioners whose primary concern is the study of higher education, but the disciplinary space is shared with many others. For all groups, and those new to the field, we provide an introductory guide to the methodology and the study of higher education.

In recent years, research has become essential to enhancing the professional learning of higher education teachers and those with administrative responsibilities in our institutions. When done well, such an activity also allows for a contribution to the knowledge and theories of the field. However, we suggest that much work is conducted by academics who have had no specific preparation in higher education research methods and the book aims to provide the guidance to help this group to improve practice. We also feel confident that those who are more established in the field can likewise benefit from an engagement with ideas around how knowledge is constructed. Overall, we wish to make an impact on the quality of higher education research.

Participation in research is also changing. First, the higher education PhD is becoming more popular, partly as a response to the maturing of a relatively young field, and partly in response to the changing nature of academic work. Second, the breakdown of traditional academic roles and new specialisms has led to more university teachers without a responsibility for disciplinary research in their discipline. For example, those on 'teaching-only' contracts can find research into practice an attractive and rational option for professional development that may also enable a contribution to be made to communities of like-minded teacher-researchers. These communities are slowly gaining legitimacy and acceptance in the sector. We argue that even a small amount of methodological knowledge and expertise will enhance the quality of research and help those interested in learning to potentially make substantive contributions to the subject and theories of higher education.

Some of the more problematic methodological concepts and research terms will be explained in the chapters that follow and guidance offered on dealing with knowledge boundaries and overlapping or competing ideas. For those entirely new to research, conceptual ideas around what 'counts' as knowledge will also be addressed. However, because learning research methodology gives epistemic access to knowledge (how disciplinary knowledge is generated), it is also particularly important when it comes to reading and critiquing published articles and theories that feed into the empirical research process. Epistemic access is also foundational to conceptual research that forms a good part of what is published in higher education.

Our overall objective is to support learning about research methodology to enable novice researchers to become more competent in research approaches and improve understanding of the seemingly unlimited possibilities for research design. We reason that methodological skill will change the quality of research and help the researcher make a better contribution to knowledge. Expertise in higher education research is part of the university knowledge project because it contributes to theory formation, enhances academic practice and ultimately improves the student learning experience. However, any research of quality must have something worthwhile to say, for both the researcher and the wider community in which they reside. In this sense, methodological understanding is essentially a quality issue.

1 The origin of the thesis

Both authors work as higher education researchers and academic developers. Like most other developers, we both started our university careers in another field before making the switch. One of us worked in pure science and the other in computer science. For both of us, the new subject of higher education was initially unfamiliar territory. We initially observed that nearly all the published research accounts that were relevant to academic development work were qualitative or using mixed methods, and of course these studies did not follow the rules and methods of science that we were used to. As a consequence, learning about qualitative inquiry became central to our work. We now have many years' experience of developing and teaching on research methods courses, mainly for postgraduate students and established academics who are research novices in the subject of higher education. Our students and colleagues come from a wide range of disciplinary backgrounds, both in New Zealand and from universities across the world.

What most of the academic novices have in common is that they already have substantial research expertise in their discipline and so can draw on this when learning about higher education research. Sometimes it is a bonus when knowledge, experience and traditions from both fields are congruent and the transition to higher education study is seamless. At other times, when the academic comes from a very different tradition, we need to work through a range of conceptual barriers. What constitutes legitimate knowledge in the new discipline can be challenging. In particular, we know that the largely qualitative study of higher education is radically different to quantitative scientific research, and that those from a quantitative tradition do not always know the numerical methods typical of the social sciences. Social science systems of higher education tend to be incredibly complex and not easily amenable to study using the rules of science. However, many scientists make a successful transition into higher education research, including the authors of this book. We are aware that our experience of scientific research, clinical trials, mixed methods research and many different forms of qualitative inquiry help us to work with our colleagues from all subject traditions. We currently mainly use qualitative methodologies to study higher education, but this depends on the research question. How we frame the qualitative-quantitative question is discussed in the next section.

In our courses, we recommend some of the major works in research methods, including Patton (2002). The texts we use are often comprehensive and insightful but are not written for a single academic discipline. Because of this, ideas frequently need to be translated and transferred to particular contexts and, in our case, the cultural and social situations of higher education. In addition, it can take many years to develop methodological expertise and those taking semester-long postgraduate courses need to get up to speed quickly. To meet such needs, this book is designed to provide an accessible account for this group. In suggesting this, we open ourselves to criticism and perhaps accusations of a 'quick fix' for a complex problem. However, it is the reality we face, as the field of study is largely made up of part-time researchers who have higher education as a secondary interest. Most are academics undertaking research into university teaching as part of their professional formation. We believe that the field needs a book that addresses the challenge of discipline specificity and one that also scaffolds the learning for a wide range of students and academics interested in the study of higher education.

2 What is research in higher education?

Lawrence Stenhouse described research as a systematic inquiry made public (Stenhouse, 1981) and we think this is an elegant and concise definition that every researcher should regularly return to. Research is not just about producing a journal article or book chapter. It is concerned with producing new knowledge and in most disciplines this can be made public in many ways. From a professional development perspective, we suggest there is value in thinking about practice or issues affecting higher education, which will occur to academics often and naturally, and taking the time to conduct a systematic inquiry to address concerns and challenges. The more rigorous this inquiry becomes, the higher the quality of the final product and the greater the likelihood that a contribution can be made to the wider academic community. We argue that the quality of ideas will be matched by the demands of the communication medium and the rigours of peer review and criticism. All readers will be able to differentiate what needs to be done for a departmental seminar compared to an international journal article. However, that is not to say there is no value in identifying a problem, carefully reflecting on it and discussing thoughts and ideas with colleagues. Beyond such initial steps towards a practice change, a certain facility with research techniques and approaches – and therefore thorough methodological understanding – is required. This is particularly the case for empirical research in higher education.

Research methods are typically framed as either quantitative or qualitative, but this categorization is not as straightforward as it seems and it has been described as a 'false dichotomy' (Rowbottom & Aiston, 2006). Most so-called quantitative research has an element of subjective interpretation and, theoretically, everything in the qualitative world can be counted to create a quantitative component. Briefly, quantitative research methods (the subject of Chapter 4) have statistically significant conclusions, may try to explain cause and effect, often move from samples to populations and so try to find results that are generalizable. This type of research may be experimental or descriptive. In contrast, qualitative research is about the subjective interpretation of a social phenomenon and it produces detailed interpretive accounts that have been described as providing 'thick description' or rich narratives. Partly to by-pass the difficult binary categorization of qualitative or quantitative research, we now have a burgeoning field of 'mixed methods' research, which is essentially about combining the two traditions and making sure several data sources are used in a study when relevant.

We know that empirical research in the field of higher education consists principally of qualitative inquiry and the vast majority of published articles in the top ranked journals would be classified in this way (Tight, 2012). Yet many of these articles contain quantitative methods. What we propose here is that it does not really matter what label is used for a study or a method, as long as the researcher has a clear question and a study is designed to answer this. The approach that the researcher then selects will determine the methods. These methods will be informed by the researcher's philosophy, the way they understand knowledge production and a host of pragmatic factors. These factors include how much money and time is available, what sort of sample size is possible, and how confident a researcher feels with a technique. For example, if a researcher has expertise in interviewing and success with this technique, then these experiences may not only feed into a preferred approach, but also direct the type of research question being asked. We recognize that such pragmatic issues can impact on the quality of knowledge production and so encourage all higher education researchers to develop wider methodological expertise and try new techniques and approaches when they feel comfortable doing so. There are nearly always alternatives in research design. However, methodological decisions should always be guided by a question, without losing sight of why the inquiry is important.

3 Data sources

This book is not exclusively conceptual although it does draw on a variety of established theories in research methodology. Many of the ideas come from working with new researchers and the stories they tell us about their experiences. In addition, we have conducted original studies about research theory that have employed empirical data collection and action research modes. Where ideas and claims rely on these empirical sources, it will be made clear how data were gathered. The book has 12 chapters and each is written to stand alone for those wishing to learn about specific topics. Nonetheless, it has a sequence from beginning to end that appears rational to us (although not everyone will necessarily share our logic). We believe that the book will provide practical and constructive support for a research methods course in higher education study and also be of use to all disciplines and traditions that use qualitative and mixed methods forms of research. A summary of each chapter follows.

Chapter 1 The study of higher education

This chapter explains the main conceptions and the values of research methods in higher education, emphasizing how the subject contributes to the scholarship of teaching and research. The subject of higher education is studied by academics from all disciplines across the university and by those who specifically have higher education as their only subject. All these researchers are essentially studying their own social situations and this raises many complex questions for the practitioner. We argue that in order to learn about research and take part in a multifaceted research community, an understanding of the broader context for research is important to provide a framework for study. The chapter has seven common topics that have been raised by academics taking part in our research methods programmes. These are:

- The higher education community
- Research as a form of teaching
- The evolution of teaching research
- The intellectual exercise of qualitative research
- Discovery
- Jargon or disciplinary language?
- Research methodology as a field of inquiry in higher education

Chapter 2 Ontology and epistemology

This chapter provides an overview of ontology and epistemology framed as a values construct or 'research philosophy', and explains why this is an important concept for researchers. We examine the ways in which ontology and epistemology are incorporated into written texts, including the research thesis and published articles in journals. In addition, some ideas about how research teams work and negotiate different philosophical positions are included. The chapter will address the nature and function of ontologies and epistemology, providing examples from our research and the literature. In this context, the idea of epistemic access is critical. With respect to empirical research, we draw on a study that examined the views of those who teach courses in research methods in higher education and how they understand the nature and purpose of ontology and epistemology.

Chapter 3   Qualitative research approaches

Study design is an important aspect of planning for any project and the researcher will need to decide which approach best meets the research question. Sometimes the answer is obvious and at other times a question can be addressed using a variety of approaches. In this chapter, the role of design will be considered and an overview provided of each of the common types of qualitative research approach. In addition, empirical, conceptual and reflective studies will be addressed with respect to how they differ, how they overlap and how they can be combined. We describe the following approaches:

- Phenomenology
- Grounded theory
- Ethnography
- Narrative inquiry

The case study (the subject of Chapter 6) is addressed briefly at this point because of its central place in higher education research design and some ideas about 'measurement scale' are introduced. We conclude the chapter with some comments on the politics of adopting a research approach.

Chapter 4   Surveys and other quantitative approaches

There are several types of quantitative approaches and we provide an overview and the core characteristics of the most common ones used in higher education. Specifically, we treat survey research with some depth but also describe experimental design and quasi-experiments. Those without a quantitative research background can use the chapter as a guide but should understand that the limited treatment of some topics is a primer for more advanced quantitative research texts. We provide a reading section at the end of the book that can be consulted for inquiry in these areas. Those familiar with quantitative approaches will be able to draw on their wider research experiences and contextualize these for work in higher education. The chapter has three sections:

- Survey approaches
- Experimental approaches
- Statistical decisions

Chapter 5   Research methods

The subject of higher education is located in the social sciences and humanities, but the topics of research interest are multi-disciplinary and sit within various disciplines. What seems clear is that most common qualitative data collection methods have been around for a long time and appear very traditional. We discuss the main methods and the various pros and cons of using each one. These are:

- Interviews and questionnaires
- Focus groups
- Video and interpersonal process recall (IPR)

We argue that because human and social conditions are changing rapidly, accepted and conventional means of data collection may need to evolve to cope with changing circumstances and address the super-complex problems that society and higher education face. As such, we conclude this chapter with some comments on mixed methods research and how the researcher should challenge methods and methodologies to ensure that methodology itself (as a field) can develop to meet the needs of research, researchers, higher education and society more broadly.

Chapter 6   The single case

Qualitative inquiry remains the dominant research methodology for articles published in the higher education journals and it is this paradigm that we mainly teach to new higher education researchers. Nearly all studies are case studies and most fall into the category of the single case. We examine the types of study that get published in higher education and use the experiences of novice researchers to identify the key sticking points when learning about case studies. These are:

1. What is the potential of the case study?
2. What forms of data are acceptable?
3. When does analysis stop?
4. What makes a quality case study?

This chapter was originally published as a research article (Harland, 2014).

Chapter 7   Research tools

In this chapter, we present an argument for keeping 'field notes' whenever a researcher undertakes a new inquiry. The idea of the field notebook is not intuitive for those learning about higher education research methods, even though they are more commonplace in science and other social science subjects. However, the field notebook is a central repository of data and a deliberative space for thinking and scholarship that can alter the quality of research. Keeping a field notebook also brings a sense of discipline and systematic rigour to the research process. Field notes can form a historical repository of ideas to provide valuable lessons, and can show how thinking has evolved over time. Finally, reflective accounts contained in field notes can be used as a valid source of data in qualitative research. We examine:

- Care of data/value and issues around quality
- Why we need to write down our observations and thoughts
- Field notes as a legitimate form of data

Chapter 8 Engaging with the literature

A literature review or analysis of prior published work forms a significant part of undertaking research. However, those new to the study of higher education find it difficult to critically engage with the literature. This chapter will examine the role of theory in the context of research methods. It will offer effective strategies for undertaking a scholarly literature review to help develop a body of knowledge (theory) and guide and shape current and future research. Despite its central role, it is a subject that has had limited attention and our experiences have suggested that few research methods programmes guide researchers in effective engagement with the literature. We draw on our methodological research into the subject of literature review and provide a 'tripartite model' aimed at systematic and critical engagement:

- Description
- Synthesis
- Critique

To illustrate the model we include examples from our teaching and tools that may help in a literature review. We conclude the chapter with some remarks on how those with more experience engage with the literature.

Chapter 9 Qualitative data analysis

Many novice qualitative researchers face significant challenges in analyzing and assessing data. The challenges are particularly acute when it comes to large volumes of interview transcripts. This chapter will provide a visual summary of the qualitative research process and discuss the decisions involved in handling data. We discuss coding and the development of themes. A framework is used that simplifies the analytical process and we make a case that analysis happens in two stages. The first is very rapid and leads to the main themes and conditional conclusions. The second stage comes during the writing, typically through a recursive process that relies on revisiting the data and theory, combined with critical and creative thinking. The two-stage approach helps the novice move ahead in a timely manner and avoids what can be an endless and stressful analytical process lasting many months. We suggest that stage one may be all that an expert requires for initial data analysis.

Chapter 10 Evaluating qualitative research

In this chapter we present an evaluative framework intended to guide researchers in how to assess the rigour of qualitative research studies. The TACT framework has four dimensions: trustworthiness, auditability, credibility and transferability. The development of TACT has been informed by various discourses on rigour in the qualitative research methods literature. TACT has been tested empirically and we present a brief account of evidence that supports its utility. TACT can serve as an important theoretical tool for setting directions for further discourses on aspects of rigour in qualitative research methodology. However, its most important function is to improve the quality of an individual's research and guide those wishing to peer review qualitative journal articles or examine a thesis.

Chapter 11 Writing for publication

What makes research special and worthy of publishing? In part, we argue that this depends on the initial question and then, at the conclusion, having 'something to say'.

In the study of higher education, like all research, the starting point is a good question that frames the inquiry, and this can be overlooked by the novice in the quest for the perfect method and study design. These ideas are applicable to interpretive work in which the researcher needs to substitute his or her original question because a better one has emerged from the study.

We have constantly seen new researchers become narrowly focused on the 'how to' while losing sight of the question. Theoretically, a question should determine the methods and sources in qualitative or mixed methods research, but we suggest that this alignment only partially represents what happens in practice (Bryman, 2007). Because the research question usually evolves and changes during the study when ideas take thinking in a new direction, the researcher should always be prepared to re-visit the question during or at the end of a study and see if it is still the most appropriate one to ask. It may have to be modified or re-written, but a question, even an evolving one, should always direct the researcher or research team and serve as the principal idea that aligns each section of the paper.

We will also look at various forms of making research public (teaching, seminars, conferences, articles) and use data to illustrate some of the issues that an author should consider before publication. We will briefly examine ideas around the act of writing, including the writing habit and language.

Chapter 12 Final words

In this brief chapter we offer final words of advice that come from reflections on writing this book and teaching research methods. These are not exhaustive nor do they form a conclusion. It would be impossible to do this for such a vast topic. What we will attempt is to say why we engage in higher education research and what we hope to achieve with this work.

Bibliography

Bryman, A. (2007). Barriers to integrating quantitative and qualitative research, *Journal of Mixed Methods Research*, 1: 8–22.

Harland, T. (2014). Learning about case study to research higher education, *Higher Education Research and Development*, 33, 6: 1113–1122.

Patton, M.Q. (2002). *Qualitative research and evaluation methods*. Thousand Oaks, CA: Sage.

Rowbottom, D.P. & Aiston, S.J. (2006). The myth of the 'scientific method' in contemporary educational research, *Journal of Philosophy of Education*, 40, 2: 137–156.

Stenhouse, L. (1981). What counts as research? *British Journal of Educational Studies*, 14, 2: 103–114.

Tight, M. (2012). *Researching higher education*. Maidenhead, UK: The Society for Research in Higher Education and Open University Press.

1

THE STUDY OF HIGHER EDUCATION

Introduction

This chapter sets the scene for the study of higher education and examines some of the current conceptions and the values of qualitative research methods. The aim is to help academics understand the broader context in the study of higher education and to provide some ideas for understanding and responding to the many questions the new researcher will need to answer. The seven topics in the chapter have emerged mainly from our research methods teaching, in particular from the conversations we have had with academics entering the field for the first time. There is no doubt in our minds that the transition from a scientific quantitative background, or a positivist view of knowledge, is a major challenge for new researchers, but the study of higher education is quite unique in the university because academics study their personal social circumstances. The aim of this chapter is to respond to the concerns and curiosity of novices in such a way as to provide some clarity around the context for higher education research. The seven topics are as follows:

1. The higher education community
2. Research as a form of teaching
3. The evolution of teaching research
4. The intellectual exercise of qualitative research
5. Discovery
6. Jargon or disciplinary language?
7. Research methodology as a field of inquiry in higher education

1 The higher education community

Who studies higher education? The answer to this question is not so straightforward but those entering the field need to know something about their new research community. Six distinct groups of people have been identified (see Table 1.1) (Harland, 2009).

Each 'partner' group has a different background but what they all have in common is an interest in the broad subject and practices of higher education, even though they might not label what they do as 'higher education'. However, confusion may arise because of a sense of place. All subjects conduct higher education research because the work is done in higher education (e.g. in a university). If a chemistry or history lecturer was asked if they did higher education research, it is likely that there would be an affirmative answer.

The first group in the table consists of education department researchers. In some way they have certain claims over the field that the others do not, partly because of education's long established history, and also because this is where the field started. These researchers typically have undergraduate or postgraduate qualifications in education and so can be seen as time-served apprentices. Group two are the professional researchers who can be located in government and specialist research institutions. Their interests typically include higher education policy and governance. Group three are the part-time researchers who make up the vast majority of researchers in the field but usually see higher education as a secondary interest. They include the historians, biologists, accountants, mathematicians and so on, who typically investigate teaching and learning within the context of their discipline. These part-time researchers have a primary research field and tend to be self-contained within their own disciplines. They have discipline-specific journals (e.g. *Journal of Accounting Education*) and conferences, or include educational streams at mainstream discipline conferences.

TABLE 1.1 People who study higher education

Group	Including
1 Education department researchers	Researchers who work in education departments and have higher education as their interest
2 Research institute professionals	Policy researchers
3 Part-time researchers	Academics from all disciplines who have a primary research subject but also do some higher education research, usually about teaching
4 Disciplinary specialists	Academics who specialize in teaching research in a single discipline
5 Academic developers	Research active academic developers
6 Administrators	University managers, administrators and support staff

The fourth group appears more rarely in the higher education community. Members of this group work in a discipline context but differ from the part-time researchers because they only do research on education in that discipline. An example from the health sciences would be 'medical education', and although we include such groups, it is debatable whether or not they would see themselves as higher education researchers. Then there are people like the authors of this book, the academic developers. Not all in this profession are researchers, but the numbers worldwide who are active is substantial enough to hold international conferences. The sixth group consists of university managers and administrators who also make contributions to higher education through specialist journals and conferences.

However, all these groups also cross boundaries and work within multidisciplinary communities such as those fostered by the Higher Education Research and Development Society of Australasia (HERDSA), the UK's Society for Research in Higher Education (SRHE), and Canada's Society for Teaching and Learning in Higher Education (STLHE). These societies provide events and conferences that bring the wider higher education group together and are the catalyst for journals that accept the whole community of researchers. When starting out, it is important to realize that, for example, the specialist nursing or geography education journals will often contain relevant, high quality articles of interest to all those who study higher education, regardless of which field of study the researchers situate themselves in.

In all of these contexts, higher education seems to be an 'open access discipline' (Harland, 2009). It appears that virtually anyone can do this work, perhaps needing only some prior research or writing skills. A background in the subject of higher education may be desirable but it is not required (Tight, 2012), and so it is inevitable that such a field sits at the bottom of the knowledge hierarchy of our institutions and society (Becher, 1989). What we argue is that the open nature of the higher education field and the diversity of researchers should be celebrated. It belongs to all those who work in higher education and have an interest in higher education's practices, regardless of what subject is normally studied or taught. However, there is a caveat, in that most of what is published seems to be descriptive accounts of practice. There are 3.7 million hits in Google Scholar for 'problem based learning' and you don't have to drill down too far to find the majority of work is essentially descriptive. We propose that many of these studies would have been of higher quality had a critical approach been taken to research and this idea is foundational to our thinking about research methodology and higher education scholarship.

2 Research as a form of teaching

> On the whole, within universities and among scholars, the status hierarchy in science attributes the highest status to basic research, secondary status to applied research, and virtually no status to formative and action research.
>
> *(Patton, 2002, p. 223)*

Patton's argument has a central idea about explaining how research is valued and we believe that this hierarchy has been sustained over time. It still carries weight and influence among the academic community, with pure or basic research having the highest status. However, the conceptual order has recently come under serious criticism. In New Zealand, the government, through research accountability exercises, has challenged the higher education sector to ensure that the research it does has some practical relevance to society. This phenomenon is part of the worldwide neoliberal shift in how governments see the relationship between universities and society and the role they have in supporting the so-called free market. Although concerns are mainly with research in STEM subjects (science, technology, engineering and mathematics) and work that has direct economic gain, there is still some room on the margins of the main argument for research that addresses 'wider' societal benefits. It is here that higher education research can claim a legitimate place, if its central purposes are considered to meet the new utility criterion and if practitioners can demonstrate the benefits and applied nature of their work.

We would contend that all research (in all subjects) is done first to help the researcher learn, then to help colleagues and peers learn and then the broader community (see Chapter 2). Research is therefore one of the purest forms of teaching. In this conception, it has practical intent and when we directly address research to the subject of higher education, utility comes from the impact it makes on teachers and other practitioners who either listen to or read the research accounts. As this research is disseminated, it can influence practice change and the quality of education for university students should improve.

Bear in mind that most university lecturers are employed as novice teachers who must learn their craft in the first years of employment through trial and error. The errors and trials can negatively impact on successive generations of students while improvements in practice during this time have the opposite effect. It goes without saying that the sector requires teachers of the highest calibre and learning from research is an essential part of academic development for both the individual and the profession. However, learning from *carrying out* research is just as important for professional learning. Learning through research into practice and recognizing 'higher education research as teaching' are foundational values that can inform every part of the research process. For example, for the authors of this book, our work is always done to contribute to theory and to help our colleagues learn about practice. In the process we improve our practices. However, we would argue that our wider impact on society is through helping to improve the quality of academic work and so the quality of student learning. Those outside the field may interpret this latter claim as an 'indirect benefit' but we would argue that if we can contribute to high quality teaching and learning, this is also the foundation of all future research across all subjects, including pure research, STEM subjects and research done directly to improve economic success.

3 The evolution of teaching research

If research at the start of the 20th century, particularly in the field of education, is examined, we can see a clear divide between theory and practice. Research was largely quantitative and theoretical, while teaching was a practical endeavour. This quantitative-theoretical legacy remained dominant in the social sciences for much of the century, even though John Dewey (1910) had rejected such dualistic thinking and challenged the distinction between theoretical and practical knowledge by proposing that the process of inquiry was the same in either construct and so could provide a unifying concept for practice (Dewey, 1938). Dewey claimed that the properties of inquiry are contained in thinking and action and the patterns of inquiry are the same for all epistemological conceptions. It does not matter if the inquirer is addressing a question in science or a problem of everyday professional practice; knowledge is formed through the inquiry process. This idea is congruent with the claim made above, that the primary purpose of research is teaching and that the outcome of learning is a practice change.

In 1946, Kurt Lewin recognized the need to legitimize practical knowledge acquired through inquiry. Lewin developed the concept of 'action research', in which a teacher identifies a problem that needs a solution and then embarks on a process of problem identification, imagining possible solutions, trying these out, systematically evaluating the outcomes and embedding change in practice. The outcomes are actionable theories that contrast with the older view that teachers should apply the theories that educational experts have developed for them:

> Research that produces nothing but books will not suffice.
> *(Lewin, 1946, p. 35)*

In the 1980s, Donald Schön explicitly re-worked Dewey's principles of inquiry and the concept of action research for professional learning and proposed the theory of reflective practice (Schön, 1987). He was interested in competence and how professionals become excellent practitioners, and suggested that we have espoused theories that we use to explain our behaviour and also tacitly held theories-in-use which are only implicit in our behaviours. The reflective practitioner focuses on bringing tacit theories-in-use into the espoused domain, and for teachers, this means systematically examining their own teaching experiences and the technical competencies, values and knowledge that underpin these. The type of reflective activity Schön promoted was not routine and it requires a clear rationale with focused and systematic reflection. As such, it is a component of any research inquiry, including action research.

In the 1990s, Boyer and colleagues created the idea of the Scholarship of Teaching and Learning (SoTL) (Boyer, 1990). It was proposed that teaching should be reconsidered in four dimensions that he described as scholarly. These were the scholarships of discovery, integration, application and teaching. Discovery is about research; integration about utilizing existing theory; application is the process of applying knowledge; and teaching is the process of teaching. In particular, the concept of 'integration' has been influential in explaining how we can bring existing theoretical knowledge into our professional enquiries about practice and, in turn, allow us to contribute quality research to the wider store of knowledge in the field of higher education.

What the sector is presently experiencing is an epistemological turn in which research becomes a form of teaching, and that teaching is a part of all genuine research. Perhaps more importantly and on a practical level, the teacher-as-researcher of their own practices has become mainstream across all disciplines. The empirical research that teacher-researchers engage in across the sector has a variety of names (e.g. reflective practice, action research, SoTL) but what all have in common is that the methods used are largely qualitative (or perhaps mixed methods). However, this practitioner research can be of the highest quality and contribute to both teaching and theory. Lewin's assertion should be re-formulated by saying that research that produces both change and books is a better way forward in contemporary higher education (see Harland, 2010).

4 The intellectual exercise of qualitative research

As the art and craft of research is learned, there also has to be a clear ontological framing. This idea is discussed in more depth in Chapter 2 but research must also be seen as an intellectual exercise that asks challenging questions of the researcher. These include:

- What are the purposes of my research?
- What am I trying to achieve?
- What do I stand for?
- What are my values and how do I live up to these in my research?

Although the authors of this book would claim that the research we do is both theoretical and applied, we hope that each piece of work shows a clear commitment to a value position. Research is never neutral and it seems better to be clear about one's values and so open these to scrutiny and criticism. If, for example, a researcher would like to see the university built on western democratic ideas about higher education or principles around equality and fairness, then these values will influence what questions are asked, how the research is conducted and how the data are analyzed and represented. In this sense, a values-critique becomes an intellectual exercise that will challenge the higher education qualitative researcher to seek clarity of purpose.

5 Discovery

We argue that description of observations and events is only acceptable when it is the platform and context for discovery, and where it helps the researcher and reader to understand the complexities of any new theory being developed or old theory being challenged. This is the point of all qualitative research and there are two obvious stages. For empirical research, these are:

1. Ask a worthwhile question; design a study; collect data; carry out an analysis; discover something new.
2. If what is discovered is worth publishing, write an article.

However, for conceptual research, 'discovery' is also the main objective. Every time researchers think they have a new idea, then this must be checked in a recursive process of theory integration to make sure that a) they have found a gap in the knowledge and b) that this gap has some significance and worth.

6 Jargon or disciplinary language?

Like the cliché about terrorists and freedom fighters, one man's jargon seems to be another's disciplinary language. When we teach research methods in higher education to academics and postgraduates from other disciplines (particularly those from quantitative science subjects) we are frequently told that the 'jargon' in articles, books and discussion can be difficult to understand. Of course this is slightly pejorative, because the same academic would describe the difficult words and expressions in their own discipline as specialist language.

There is an assumption that it is the teacher's job to make learning straightforward, coupled with the idea that research methods in higher education can be learned quickly. Such learning contrasts markedly with the long apprenticeship typically required for a subject that includes three years of undergraduate study and up to seven years as a postgraduate. When academics develop an interest in higher education as a second field, or students come to do a PhD in higher education (there is no undergraduate route into higher education study), they seem to expect a shorter route to success. Typically, expectations will be of months rather than years. In some ways, these demands are not unreasonable and higher education programmes are set to cater for a range of disciplinary backgrounds and abilities. It is generally held (which can be partly justified) that once an academic has facility with research in his or her first field, many skills can be transferred to the study of higher education. At the same time, educational research requires vast amounts of critical reading, frequently in related and disparate subject areas. Higher education research tends to be multidisciplinary and acquiring epistemological access to relevant knowledge fields is a life-long endeavour.

7 Research methodology as a field of inquiry in higher education

What academics and students repeatedly tell us is not only that they find the broader academic literature hard to follow, but also that the methods literature is dense and full of jargon. Yet research methodology is a subject in itself and not only important for those researching higher education. The field of qualitative research methodology (to which this book also aims to contribute) is highly contestable, but essential to how knowledge can advance. As methodology tends to be a contested field, a constant lack of agreement between methodologists can be seen variously as positive (we need critiques of ideas), disabling (what to believe?) and generally frustrating for a novice researcher needing clarity and guidance. One person's 'model' is another's 'paradigm' and the two terms are (or are not) compatible. In this genuine example, we have had to justify to a peer reviewer why we have used one term rather than the other (in our view, an irritating exercise). However, such experiences have made us acutely aware of the language problems of research methods and methodology, and we have written this book in as plain English as possible, so that most academics will be able to understand our ideas and arguments without difficulty.

Bibliography

Becher, T. (1989). *Academic tribes and territories: Intellectual enquiry and the cultures of disciplines.* Milton Keynes, UK: Open University Press.
Boyer, E.L. (1990). *Scholarship reconsidered: Priorities of the professoriate.* Princeton, NJ: The Carnegie Foundation for the Advancement of Teaching.
Dewey, J. (1910). *How we think.* Boston, MA: D.C. Heath Publishers.
Dewey, J. (1938). *Logic: The theory of inquiry.* New York, NY: Henry Holt and Company.
Harland, T. (2009). People who study higher education, *Teaching in Higher Education*, 14, 5: 579–582.
Harland, T. (2010). Practitioner action research for studying higher education and improving the quality of teaching, *Malaysian Journal of Learning and Instruction*, 7: 1–14.
Lewin, K. (1946). Action research and minority problems, *Journal of Social Issues*, 2: 34–46.
Patton, M.Q. (2002). *Qualitative research and evaluation methods.* Thousand Oaks, CA: Sage.
Schön, D. (1987). *Educating the reflective practitioner.* San Francisco, CA: Jossey-Bass Publishers.
Tight, M. (2003). *Researching higher education.* Maidenhead, UK: The Society for Research in Higher Education and Open University Press.

2
ONTOLOGY AND EPISTEMOLOGY

Introduction

Salman Rushdie learned that:

> stories were not true ... but by being untrue they could make him feel and know truths that the truth could not tell him, and second, ... they all belonged to him ...
>
> *(Rushdie, 2012, p. 19)*

As research methods educators we devote considerable time to discussing ontology and epistemology with new higher education researchers. We do this because the execution of a higher education research project depends on the researcher or research team's ontological and epistemological positions. In fact, we would go further and claim that all research, including pure science, starts with underlying assumptions about a phenomenon that depend on ontology and epistemology, even when these are inaccessible to the conscious mind.

We are also aware that most new researchers find these concepts complex, not least because there is no fixed definition or even expert agreement on what they are. In fact, it is easy to find conflicting and competing definitions of both ontology and epistemology, and so the task of coming to understand what either might mean in the context of one's own research ambitions can be frustrating. The next problem is that knowing about something, and then working out how one knows about it is difficult, or perhaps even impossible, because they are experienced as one and the same thing, and so trying to separate ontology and epistemology inevitably brings any analysis to a stop (see, for example, Feyerabend, 1975).

So against this background, new researchers are likely to question why they need to embark on the task of understanding ontology and epistemology and what purpose this serves. These are challenges that become most acute when there is a requirement for the researcher to be explicit about his or her ontological and epistemological position. Such a situation is typically found when a postgraduate student is working towards a master's or PhD degree, certainly in the field of higher education.

As a starting point, we suggest a helpful way of thinking about ontology and epistemology is to recognize that all thought has deep philosophical roots that manifest as a set of value-constructs that inform our actions and beliefs about the world and about knowledge (van Manen, 1998). Ontology is synonymous with our personal beliefs, views and values, and epistemology is about the procedures we use to come to know something. In this framing, each concept is linked and principally describes what is valued and how values inform decisions and actions. With respect to conducting research, they can be called our 'research philosophy'. Accordingly, as the novice researcher studies research methods and learns how to carry out research, values are taken into account so that personal preferences and conceptions of research become explicit. These arguments can be illustrated most easily for qualitative research because at every stage of the research process, personal interpretation is required. In this context, every decision the researcher makes is based on his or her values.

Many qualitative methodologists see the act of making explicit the association between values and action as essential, in part to legitimize the path taken through the huge number of possibilities for creating knowledge in a world where purely quantitative research is seen as hierarchically superior. The structure of a qualitative research account found in a thesis, book chapter or journal article tends to be organized like a quantitative 'scientific article', but it will always have an underlying narrative form because the content is constructed through the imagination of the researcher and carefully represented for the reader. To write in such a way in qualitative research requires the researcher (or research team) to filter and interpret conceptual ideas and empirical data. No two researchers will come to exactly the same interpretation and each part of the account depends on an individual's ontological and epistemological values, even within a research team. In turn, readers will construct their own interpretation of the story they have just read because they will also have an ontological and epistemological stance.

The researcher's values are nearly always hidden in the text and, when it comes to journal articles, hardly ever made explicit. On the rare occasions when there is an attempt to be open and incorporate some explanation of ontology and epistemology in an article, it tends to be cursory and so of dubious benefit to anyone. The point here is that a researcher only needs to address ontology and epistemology to gain a better understanding of what research is, in terms of its values and aims; what is permissible; how to judge if it is of high quality; or to learn how to challenge culturally determined methodological boundaries when necessary. Once a new higher education researcher can comfortably work with these reflexive aspects of research, then he or she may only ever need to revisit ontology and epistemology when they seek to explore different ways of asking and answering research questions, or when they come across research done in an entirely new way.

There are further considerations for the qualitative researcher. First, there are different ontological concerns for empirical research (in this case defined as research that collects and analyzes original data) and conceptual research (that tends to depend on published theory as a source for developing new concepts). Second, research teams will often come up against internal and conflicting ontological and epistemological positions when designing a project and, especially, when interpreting empirical or theoretical data. Third, it is important to consider that work of the highest quality appears to be carried out and published by researchers who may or may not have consciously or explicitly engaged with ontology or epistemology: there is no way to be sure.

Given these opening comments, in this chapter we are primarily concerned with the qualitative or mixed methods research paradigms. We ask the fundamental question of whether or not an explicit focus on ontology and epistemology is essential or necessary to assist the novice in becoming a better researcher, or to improve the quality of research for those who already have research skills. In addition, we address the situation of research teams and collaborations that are very common in the study of higher education. How do they negotiate a mutual research philosophy or requirement for writing explicitly about ontology and epistemology?

The chapter has four parts:

1   An overview of ontology and epistemology framed as a values construct or 'research philosophy', and why this is an important concept for researchers.
2   An examination of the way in which ontology and epistemology are incorporated into written text, including the research thesis and published articles in journals.
3   Some ideas about how research teams work and negotiate different philosophical positions.
4   Ontology and epistemology as epistemic access to knowledge.

1 Ontology and epistemology

'My research philosophy is ...?'

Ontology is broadly understood as the study of 'being' and the nature of reality, and a system of belief and interpretation of what constitutes knowledge or reality. It is also associated with the question of whether knowledge needs to be perceived as objective or subjective. It can be argued that the choices we make in any inquiry are the essence of a 'research philosophy' because all ideas are based on our values, whether they are explicit or something held deeply that we are not aware of. Conceptions of what constitutes knowledge, with corresponding ways of knowing, are called ontology and epistemology. While ontology refers to the nature of beliefs, views and values that one holds about a specific body of knowledge and particular ways of knowing, epistemology refers to scientific procedures (including tools, processes and techniques), used to investigate a problem, whether through empirical (grounded in data) or logical and philosophical (conceptual or theoretical) research. In this sense, ontology is concerned with what there is to know and epistemology is about how we can come to know it.

Michael Polanyi (1958) described two types of knowledge. Knowledge that is tangible (explicit knowledge) and can be described using heuristics, mathematical axioms or theories, and inherent knowledge (implicit knowledge) which might not be directly captured or standardized but rather based on personal experiences and intuition. These are sometimes thought of in the context of objective and subjective forms of knowledge.

Objectivity

- Social entities exist in reality external to social actors concerned with their existence (Saunders et al., 2009).
- Meaning exists independently of social actors (Bryman & Bell, 2003, p. 22).

Subjectivity

- Social phenomena and their meanings are continually being created and accomplished by social actors, e.g. constructionism (Bryman & Bell, 2003, p. 23).
- Social phenomena are created from perceptions and consequential actions of actors concerned with their existence.

For either explicit or implicit knowledge, ontology and epistemology are two faces of the same coin, since to know about knowledge is also to understand ways of knowing. This dual structural-functional role enables us to describe and interpret knowledge, whether this ability is explicitly understood or not. It also provides us with a common language to communicate and evaluate knowledge (see Section 4 below) in order to understand either the material or immaterial world. Viewed in another way, both ontology and epistemology are theoretical levels of abstraction that guide researchers to maintain a balance of logic and rigour throughout a research process. They offer a rationale and tools to standardize different and often incompatible ways of producing knowledge, and also provide consumers of knowledge with some grounds on which to value and trust the quality of research outcomes.

Because there are many different ways of describing how we come to know something and understand knowledge, as well as different meanings and explanations for ontology and epistemology, there is a complexity that can challenge those new to higher education research. In order to simplify the task in our research methods courses, we have found that Jonathan Grix's conceptual work for beginning researchers in the social sciences provides an accessible account and suitable foundation (Grix, 2002). This author suggests that there is interdependence and a

The interrelationship between the building blocks of research

Ontology	Epistemology	Methodology	Methods	Sources
What's out there to know?	What and how can we know about it?	How can we go about acquiring that knowledge?	Which precise procedures can we use to acquire it?	Which data can we collect?

FIGURE 2.1 The building blocks of research (after Grix, 2002)

direct relationship between ontology, epistemology and sources of data and methods. He proposes that ontology is foundational to epistemology, and that both direct us to sources of data and then methods. In other words, our values and how we see the world are essential to how we understand knowledge and how we go about producing it (see Figure 2.1).

In Grix's interpretation, the choices we make are the essence of ontology. Interrogating one's own ontological position is an exercise in examining values that influence all subsequent research decisions. If we have some clarity around these values, in theory, this knowledge will help to improve the quality of research. The reader of a research account can accept that an article contains a certain ontological position, whether stated or not, and the premise that this can be either fully or partly deduced (if we put our mind to it). Although the linear relationship has proved very useful for teaching research methods, we argue that ontology and epistemology are logically interdependent concepts. In addition, the linearity of Grix's model describes a single series of steps in a progressive process that has no feedback component to allow adjustment at each stage. The arrow in Figure 2.1 is there to show how one building block informs the next. However, what is likely to happen is that new understanding at each stage feeds back into the whole methodological process.

We also know that for many researchers, an explicit ontological foundation will not be of concern, and that most published research accounts have to be read at face value. In addition, any ontological assumptions the reader might make (e.g. about the writer's values) will be personal to them. It is well established that two different researchers using the same methods to answer the same question, but from a different ontological perspective, will almost certainly come up with different interpretations and conclusions. The same reasoning applies to readers. In addition, if a full and explicit methodological treatment of ontology and epistemology is included in a research account, there is no guarantee that different readers would even agree on the appropriateness of the treatment itself.

In qualitative empirical research, it is frequently suggested that authors should provide some explanation of the outcomes of decisions so that readers can better understand and judge the worth of the narratives constructed. This explanatory task becomes an exercise in examining the values that inform what the researcher is trying to achieve and communicate. In other words, describing the stance, purpose or argument. Yet if higher quality thinking and higher quality research is not achieved through this process, then there seems little practical utility in pursuing such an explicit task. At present, the relationship between an explicit account of ontology and epistemology and research quality is not well understood. However, the generally accepted argument is that a deep engagement with these ideas has the potential to help new researchers to improve research skills and knowledge, and on the basis of this change, the quality of new subject knowledge and theory. Yet we have colleagues with similar roles to ours who would not share such a view and who do not tackle ontology and epistemology in research training. So why do we defend the teaching of ontology and epistemology, when presently there seems to be little evidence for the link between these ideas and the quality of research?

We suggest that if there were some general principles that could underpin all qualitative empirical and conceptual research, then the higher education field would move closer to the empiricism and perceived certainty of pure science. The scientific method is generally assumed to have a shared ontological and epistemological understanding (even when this is not true). If there was a single equivalent qualitative position, then the researcher and reader could make similar assumptions without further effort or excessive introspection. However, qualitative ideas need constant renewal and clarification each time a new study is conducted, partly because subjectivity and natural bias are yet to be fully accepted in research, but also to contribute to the quality of thought and ideas. This contribution comes from a creative and critical process that interrogates subjectivity.

In addition, because many qualitative articles published in the field of higher education are conceptual (Harland, 2012), they do not have the equivalent methods section of an empirical study and so there is usually no space for methodology. We argue that all writers think and position themselves because a range of values come into play with every decision made, but the question remains whether these should be made explicit in a conceptual research account. And if so, what depth of explanation is required?

Research paradigms

Another way of learning about ontology and epistemology is to claim a research paradigm that correlates with certain ontological and epistemological positions. In approaching the problem this way, the new researcher can choose a paradigm that suits their purposes and then adopt the corresponding ontology and epistemology. These typical paradigms are shown in Table 2.1.

There are alternative paradigms to these and alternative ontological and epistemological explanations. The variety of explanations is not just semantic or related to how others might understand and explain these concepts. In fact, as claimed earlier, it is possible to find both ontology and epistemology defined using similar

TABLE 2.1 Five research paradigms with foundational knowledge values

Paradigm	Ontology	Epistemology
Positivism	An objective testable reality	Testable theories of knowledge
Critical realism	An objective reality that may not be testable	Individual understanding of reality
Interpretive	Reality created by the individual	Knowledge unique to the individual
Critical theory	Reality is socially constructed and interested	Knowledge not separated from power
Pragmatism	Reality is driven by experience	Knowledge needs to have utility

words. This situation provides quite a challenge for the novice. In this context, the 'paradigm approach' will be seen by some as a good starting point to help them understand why and how knowledge might be constructed. Even though this path to ontology and epistemology is at a high level of abstraction, it is nevertheless a viable route. If adopted, several related questions will need to be addressed:

1 Are any of the paradigms exclusive?
2 Can a researcher adopt a single paradigm and then ensure that deeper and more personal ideas about ontology and epistemology correspond?
3 Does it impede reflexive ideas about cause and effect?

Where we feel the paradigm approach has most utility is for research carried out by a research team. The reason we make this claim is that negotiating ontology and epistemology among several researchers is likely to be fraught with problems (discussed in Section 3 of this chapter). As a further caveat, we would add that even if a paradigm approach is a possibility, it might not be desirable because the primary focus in any research always needs to be on the research question. There is no logical reason why a qualitative or mixed-methods researcher cannot design a project that includes, to some degree, more than one of the above paradigms, and such flexibility around paradigms might allow for a better approach to answer a question, especially when there are multiple aims for a project. What might be called a mixed methods research design typically relies on multiple forms of knowing but not multiple ontologies.

If there were some general principles to underpin all qualitative and conceptual higher education research that did not need renewal or clarification each time work was published, again the field would move closer to the empiricism and certainty of pure science and the scientific method. As already argued, the scientific method generally assumes a shared ontology and epistemology, and if there was a single qualitative position, then the researcher and reader could make similar assumptions without further effort and excessive introspection or reflexivity. This position could be called relativist, but even from a limited exposure to reading or carrying out qualitative research, it is fairly easy to accept that both producers and consumers of research can share a variety of ideas about, for example, truth and the validity of claims being made.

With respect to paradigms, quantitative research tends to be aligned with positivism and qualitative research with interpretivism (Table 2.1). In Figure 2.2 we show some of the characteristics of quantitative and qualitative research, but position mixed methods between these positions.

Quantitative	Mixed methods	Qualitative
Universalistic	....	Relativistic
Atomistic	....	Holistic
Deductive	....	Inductive
Nomothetic	....	Idiographic
Explanatory	....	Descriptive/exploratory
Hypothesis driven	....	Speculative/illustrative
Abstract	....	Grounded
Objective	....	Subjective
Imposes theory	....	Exposes actors' meanings
Standardized	....	Moving target
Value-free	....	Political
Rigorous	....	Non-rigorous
Number-crunching	....	Story-telling
Experimental	....	Naturalistic

FIGURE 2.2 Ontological and epistemological features of methodology

We then go one step further to provide a paradigmatic model that links positivism to mainly quantitative traditions, interpretivism to mainly qualitative traditions and pragmatism to mainly mixed methods traditions (see Figure 2.3).

One of the reasons for including statements about ontology and epistemology in written accounts is to help the reader (sometimes an examiner) to gain access to a researcher's or research team's value decisions. However, while helping a reader understand the choices made, each reader will still interpret the work in a different way. It is a moot point if explanation and direction will significantly alter how the work is seen and understood, and it is unknown whether or not this adds value beyond providing a relatively complete methodological rationale. For example, ontology and epistemology can explain why critical realism rather than pragmatism was used as a research paradigm, but for those wanting to engage with what the work has to say, rather than how the work was done, such details may have limited utility.

On the other hand, the qualitative research community has invested a great deal of thought in describing the concepts and values that underpin qualitative research in order to help new researchers. From the methodologists' perspective such an understanding is central to becoming a researcher. In other words, researchers need to fully understand methodology and the arguments behind ontology

```
                    Epistemological stance

Quantitative tradition  ←  Positivism      Interpretivism  →  Qualitative tradition

                           Pragmatism
```

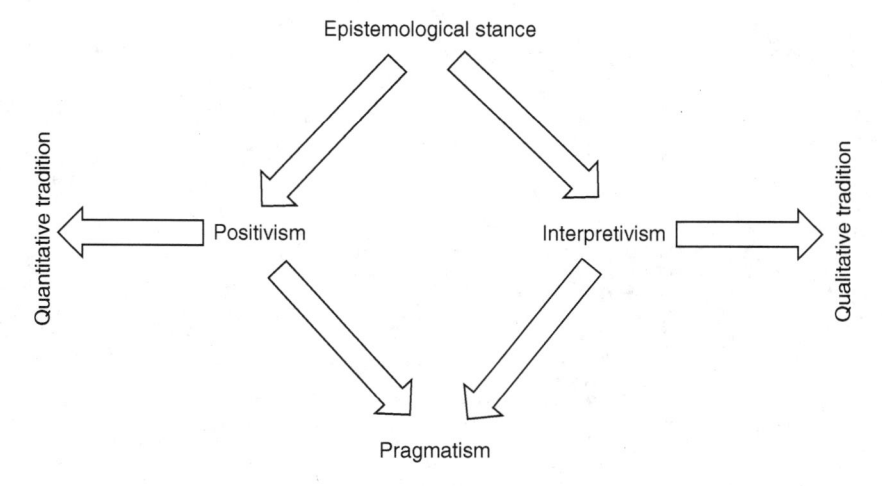

FIGURE 2.3 The three main traditions of research and their relationship

and epistemology, even if they later wish to reject or by-pass these in the research process and publication. What the research community currently lacks is evidence about the differences inclusion makes and what might happen to the field if explicit ontological and epistemological statements were universally adopted. At present, we know that there is much high quality research already published that gives no clue about the level of methodological understanding of the writer or research team. The general assumption seems to be that the expert will already know these things and does not have to make them explicit.

2 How ontology and epistemology are made explicit

When is an explicit written ontology and epistemology required? The evidence suggests that this is a once in a lifetime obligation when writing a master's or PhD thesis. Afterwards, it seems possible to continue as a higher education researcher without having to formally address these concepts again in any detail. However, not all those who study higher education will have postgraduate qualifications in the higher education field or in any other educational or sociological subject area. Yet a cursory glance at published research articles shows successful researchers who do not explicitly address ontology and epistemology or make statements or claims about these concepts in their work. We know some of these researchers personally and respect their work. Again, the question needs to be asked if explicit ontological and epistemological accounts change the quality of the research. If a researcher or research team have included a section on ontology or epistemology in their methods, how might this alter the quality of the paper and the reader's experience? If explicit philosophical engagement became a journal requirement, would there also be a risk that it becomes no more than a form of legitimization that gives the impression of thoroughness and rigour in the work?

TABLE 2.2 Research types published in two major higher education journals

Research type	Research philosophy stated	Research philosophy not stated	Total
Conceptual	1	157	158
Empirical	11	433	444
Total	**12**	**590**	**602**

We investigated the current practices of researchers who published empirical and conceptual articles in two high-ranking higher education journals to see if and how the inclusion of explicit statements about ontology and epistemology were managed. In addition, we examined a selection of postgraduate higher education theses. Between 2010 and 2013, 602 articles were published in two of the major higher education journals, *Teaching in Higher Education* and *Studies in Higher Education* (see Harland, 2014). The articles were divided into two categories of empirical and conceptual. The empirical category consisted of research that specified a method and the researchers collected data for analysis. The conceptual category consisted of a range of other research types including essays and reviews. These conceptual articles did not specify a method. For this exercise, ontology and epistemology were abbreviated as 'research philosophy'. The results are shown in Table 2.2.

Twelve articles had some form of brief ontological or epistemological statement. One addressed only ontology and another only epistemology. Eleven did this in a single sentence while one used two sentences. This data suggests that inclusion is a very rare practice in journal articles and that any claims are very brief. It seems clear that there is no requirement for being explicit on these matters. It may simply be that most qualitative research is learned through trial and error and not through methodological study, and, according to Seale (1999), is a 'craft occupation'.

The data in Table 2.2 could also be explained by the space limitations of journals driving certain behaviour. In a postgraduate thesis, space is flexible and so allows for a thorough account of ontology and epistemology, whereas the tight word limit of a journal article does not easily permit this. It may also be extremely difficult to say anything meaningful or useful about ontology and epistemology without overwhelming a 6,000-word article and putting the text out of balance. Similar arguments may apply to other publication formats including books, book chapters and conference papers. We know that in a thesis, it can take many pages to fully describe one's ontology and epistemology, for both the exercise itself and what follows in the thesis to have any meaning at all. Of course, a PhD student also has the advantage of being a single researcher.

If these observations have some validity, then could attempts to include an ontological statement in qualitative or mixed methods journal articles be seen as tokenism or a response to perceived social and cultural demands? Put another way, is the researcher trying to attain some form of 'equivalence' to science methodology through trying to be explicit? In this situation, statements of ontology and epistemology would serve very little purpose beyond the pseudo-legitimization of knowledge creation. On the other hand, efforts to include a research philosophy may genuinely be for the benefit of readers, in order to help them understand the researcher's knowledge construction and knowledge claims. Higher education research has an audience outside the research field itself (though with an interest in higher education), and some may be more used to the scientific quantitative paradigm with its rationality and objectivity, causal relationships and generalizability. A full methodological treatment in qualitative research may also help these readers.

The postgraduate students we supervise value the opportunity to develop a research philosophy as part of a full methodological argument that is normally included in a thesis chapter entitled 'Methodology'. Once students acquire some appreciation of the concept, the exercise gives them a clearer understanding of how knowledge is constructed in both qualitative and mixed methods research, and in particular, how their personal values influence both their positionality and every step of the research process. This understanding can take several years to arrive at and ideas are typically refined right up to the point of thesis submission.

A level of introspection is required for this values-driven task that could also be seen, in part, as therapeutic. For example, Cousin (2010) is concerned about 'positional piety' when affinity with research subjects is claimed. She gives the case of working-class women studying working-class women as subjects. Here there is potential to claim that an ontological position is virtuous because of affinity. When an ontological statement drifts into unnecessary confession, the supervisor may have to advise students to moderate their writing. This is harder for a supervisor than one might imagine, as there is often strong emotional investment in writing this reflexive component of a methodology chapter. Yet a researcher's philosophical stance does require deep reflection about values formed over time and the process of reflecting on ontological formation can help to clearly define what motivates the individual to do the research in the first place. It allows a well-thought-out rationale and purpose to be formulated and 'purposeful research' is likely to be more engaging and better quality. We shall return to this idea in the final chapter. Bruce Macfarlane (2016) warns, however, that writing built on reflexive self-awareness can become a form of emotional performativity, especially if students believe their supervisor expects this. An introspective account that reveals unnecessary personal information or feelings is likely to get in the way of developing a research philosophy.

Writing for a referee

A full methodology may be appropriate for a postgraduate thesis and expected by a supervisor and examiner; however, writing for a referee in a journal is different. We have both had personal experiences of writing a short philosophical statement in the introduction or methods section of an article, and on every occasion it has been fraught with problems, because the referees that we have encountered (who seem to have an interest in such methodological issues or simply feel able to express an alternate opinion) tend to critique this section and create nearly impossible situations, from which we have had great difficulty trying to extract ourselves. In our experience, and that of all our research colleagues across the world, without exception, it is seen as a dangerous thing to do.

Methodological savvy referees will want concepts explained further and may even require some terms to be exchanged with others: for example, one referee might argue that an 'approach' should be a 'paradigm' (a real case). We have also had papers rejected on methodological grounds that went on to be published without revision in other journals, and so inclusion can become a lottery characterized by a semantic exchange in a situation of unequal power. We advise our students and new researchers to be very economical with what they say so as not to open such a debate. Even a simple statement such as 'this is an ethnographic study' is better avoided. Avoidance allows the referee to ask for more detail and, so far, our advice has not led to a) any rejection of work based on lack of methodological depth, or b) any requests for fuller explanation. Because others across the higher education field may already understand this, it might explain why there is only one attempt at including two sentences on ontology and epistemology in 602 articles. We suggest that most researchers will quickly learn to emulate what is 'normal' for their field and specific journals or, if they have had similar experiences to us during our 'naive' period, stop attempts to include fuller methodological explanations.

In some ways, we could be seen as slow learners but as enthusiastic research methodologists, because we cling to the idea that fuller methodological accounts should have the effect of contributing to better quality research outcomes, partly through challenging the established boundaries for knowledge representation in higher education research. We have no evidence that this idea holds true. We both referee for a wide range of higher education journals and make a point of being open-minded about how research is designed and conducted. For those papers that we recommend for acceptance (usually when they have something worthwhile to contribute – see Chapter 11), we find very little included that is specific to ontology or epistemology. It seems that discussions around 'meaning making', how we come to know something, and what knowledge is, is presently left to the postgraduate research apprentice, those with an interest in research methods, and perhaps the philosophers who study these subjects. These circumstances may be true in terms of explicit declarations, but implicitly a peer reviewer or experienced reader should be able to determine something about an author's research philosophy from the methods, analysis and claims.

3 How research teams work and negotiate different philosophical positions

If a PhD student or new researcher is required or encouraged to start thinking about their philosophical stance towards research and knowledge construction, then it would be unreasonable to think ideas can be formed over a short space of time or without much experience of actually doing research. For the individual, a research philosophy is likely to take many years to refine and only after deep engagement with the subject and its practices. With new experiences, a philosophy will surely change. If this task is a complex undertaking for the individual, then how does the idea of ontology and epistemology impact on research outcomes when several researchers come together to form a research team? In addition, research teams are not necessarily stable over time and members will change. In our study of journal articles, four out of the 12 that included ontology or epistemology were single authored. It seems then that teams can carry out research and in the resulting publication write one or two sentences that the reader can assume they have all agreed on.

When the articles in these journals were examined, we decided to try and imagine what might go in the methods section of a new article on the subject of ontology and epistemology, and how we might include a joint methodological statement in the methods section. Co-writing this retrospective piece was neither a practical nor theoretical option, so we started by constructing post hoc personal accounts with the purpose of sharing them, and then negotiating and editing a text that would lead to a single short paragraph for an article that would satisfy both of us. The following was our first attempt:

BEN

My ontological and epistemological position, whether in consumption of research output or in production of it, is influenced by domain factors (my education and training), and personal factors (experiences). This position acknowledges the philosophical diversity and debate on the issues around ontological and epistemological semantics, while maintaining a pragmatic approach to a particular research methodology and problems those methodologies are set to address. In taking this position, I also acknowledge the role of epistemology and ontology in shaping the process of research as well as the quality of its outcome.

TONY

I am essentially a Deweyian pragmatist, and when I see a problem that I am curious about, and that would be useful to research, and that is novel, then I may start an inquiry. Good research is about choosing the right question and making a contribution to a field by having 'something to say'. My quest is new knowledge, first for myself, then for my readers, and then for a wider audience of those involved in universities and broader society. This new knowledge is a moveable feast in that it can only come about in one context at a moment in time. I tend to have a constructivist outlook, but also regard myself as a realist from time to time, or a critical realist, or whatever seems to fit when I am thinking and reading in this methodological area. Sometimes I feel like an ethnographer studying people and culture, but my peers have told me that my research does not fit this type of systematic study. I have never worked out why this is so.

What is foundational to my ontology is interpretation and hermeneutics. I construct the knowledge by interpreting the experiences and narratives of

> those who help me in my research. I see knowledge and theory encapsulated in experience in a particular field, and I see that experience difficult to recount and not easily measured, however we think of the meaning of the term 'measurement'. I work in super-complex worlds of social human thought and action. I am a boundary transgressor and cross into many fields outside of higher education, without ever being the same expert in those subjects. However, I learn from them and draw ideas in a trans-disciplinary act of open piracy. I use the term 'open' because I never hide my sources, but celebrate them – a kind of ontological pride.

Returning to these accounts after a period of reflection we felt it would be too difficult to go any further with the exercise. It seemed that our very different attempts were written at quite a high level of abstraction and were too vague to be of use for a reader critiquing any research design or conceptual paper. As such, they lacked any technical or procedural connection to our imagined research approach. Both appeared 'false' in the sense that we were making broad values statements that came from experiences of already completed research projects, and so described our commonly practised procedures, data collection and analysis, or conceptual essays. In fact, we concluded that we would simply continue to start all projects with a question and choose approaches and methods before reflecting on ontological justifications (and only if it was required of us).

Another reason for difficulty in this exercise was that most of the words we chose to use, along with every construct, required fuller explanation and further discussion. We might have been able to complete this task eventually but it would have been daunting. We could not imagine doing this with a research team of three or four when negotiating a research question or in the early part of project design. Yet the reflexive exercise was not futile, because we learnt something about each other for the first time after working closely for a number of years. We found that we had much in common and as we discussed the implicit and explicit values in our short statements, we could see how these influenced some of our thinking about our current research. Perhaps this is the main benefit for the PhD or master's student when research methods are studied and ideas about research, knowledge and values need to be made explicit in writing.

> Reading and discussing such methodological ideas, then, is a sort of intellectual muscle-building exercise, time out in the brain gymnasium, before returning to the task at hand, hopefully a little stronger and more alert.
>
> *(Seale, 1999, p. 475)*

4 Epistemic access

Ontology and epistemology are not just about informing one's own research, but help to understand the work of others. Of course these two ideas are closely related, but a novice often separates 'doing' research and 'reading' research accounts. It has been reasoned that to understand specialized theoretical knowledge a researcher needs to learn the generative principles of disciplinary knowledge and we maintain that this includes a thorough understanding of methodology. Knowing how knowledge is constructed has been termed 'epistemic access'. It helps the researcher understand 'how' one might come to know something in a field. Morrow (2009) describes epistemic access as:

> Gaining access, thus, was learning how to become a participant in practice, and since academic practices have developed around the search for knowledge, access to an academic practice entailed epistemological access.
> *(Morrow, 2009, p. 70)*

We would go further than Morrow and suggest that ontological access is also required, along with competence in methods and sources (Grix, 2002). Leesa Wheelahan (2014) adds that epistemic access allows a way into a system of meaning making that can provide a new understanding of the debates and controversies in a subject. This shift in thinking about ontology and epistemology is crucial because it takes the concept away from the postgraduate's PhD thesis methodology or the researcher's research study methods, and provides a different rationale for a deep engagement. In this interpretation, learning about ontology and epistemology will allow the researcher to interpret the broader theories and published articles they read in a more critical manner, and gain new and different insights. Then, new thoughts and ideas feed back into the researcher's work through an iterative and what is an essentially creative process.

Conclusion

Epistemology and ontology can be understood as a 'research philosophy' or more simply as a set of values that drive all research project decisions. Understanding epistemology or ontology can be problematic because these are both rather abstract concepts that lack a simple or agreed meaning. As such, they can be extremely difficult to understand for those starting to develop knowledge and expertise, especially in qualitative or mixed methods research. We question whether or not 'interest' in the study of methodology is enough of a reason for methodologists to expect it from others outside of this theoretical field. In other words, it might be acceptable for a theorist to engage with these ideas, but should a new higher education researcher spend this time and, if so, what are the benefits?

In addition, there are few written examples available to the new researcher. The practice seems to be specific to formal research training for higher education (and other social sciences) and postgraduate study. Even then, examples will be at a rudimentary stage as the novice comes to grip with how they see the world, how they understand knowledge and how these relate to methods (and every other step of their research project). Ideas about research develop over time, through experience and with a constant re-examination of the core values and concepts of methodology. Research team members are unlikely to share the same ontology or reasons for doing the research in the first place.

There are many other problems with research ontology and epistemology. It is difficult to connect any written accounts with what a reader learns from a study, and as such the link between ontological and epistemological explicitness and research quality has never been proven. It would be interesting to see, for example, if a journal that insisted on a full methodological exposition would in fact be able to show higher quality research outcomes. We somehow doubt this would be the case (there are many quality published articles without this demand) and the practical and commercial considerations of publishers would make it demanding, simply because of the cost of space and page limitations. Of course, online journals could match unlimited digital space with methodological exposition. This could be done in the form of appendices if it made the article too long, or if epistemology and ontology was of limited reader interest.

It might even be possible to have a digital repository of research philosophies that could be written once, and then updated by the researcher as they develop thinking in this area. These could be referenced in all the researcher's future articles, whether in print or online journals. Such a worldwide digital repository or 'register' of higher education researchers' ontological and epistemological positions would be 'living'. As researchers' career progress and their ideas change, they could update their statements. Researcher accounts would be searchable by anyone interested and could serve two other purposes. First, the database could come to represent the philosophical thinking that underpins the field, and second it could provide examples for the novice researcher and postgraduate student to help them understand the production of knowledge through qualitative and mixed methods research.

In the meantime, we will continue to teach research methodology and work with our postgraduate students in the same manner as we have always done. Our assumptions are that coming to grips with why and how knowledge is shaped by values helps students to:

- articulate their thinking;
- justify decisions as the research develops;
- gain new perspectives on knowledge; and
- read and understand published research accounts.

The task, however, is very challenging for the emerging researcher, because it requires theoretical understanding of the concepts as they apply in various ways to the design of the study, collection of data, connections to wider theory, and the ultimate research conclusions. In contrast to the postgraduate student thesis, the obligation to explain the research process does not seem to apply to the journal article (where the same material might also be presented). A cursory examination of higher education journals shows that few contain an explicit treatment of ontology and epistemology while most have nothing at all. However, articles have 'implicit' treatment and epistemic access may allow extrapolation from the text to an approximate ontology and epistemology.

Once this part of a postgraduate researcher's formal education is completed, we argue that some new ontological and epistemological understanding then becomes incorporated in any future research, whether or not explanations for the outcomes of methodological decisions are given. In this sense, the exercise of having to think about how knowledge comes into being has utility in itself and raises many questions. For example:

- Why am I asking this research question and not another?
- What am I trying to achieve through publishing my research?
- What difference does my research make?

We suggest that methodological conversations should continue even when the formal requirement for written accounts of ontology and epistemology are not necessary. However, for the thesis student, we regard answering such questions as mandatory. Even if the process does not result in ontological and epistemological clarity, it helps the novice come to an understanding of the many different dimensions of qualitative and mixed methods approaches.

As far as including such accounts in journals goes, our counsel would be to respect the 'interpretive turn' in research development and simply tell your story well and leave it to others to make it their own. Writers have less control than they may wish when it comes to what the reader will take away, as the reader has his or her own ontological and epistemological standpoint. This fact does not mean that the researcher should not have a clear argument or seek to influence others, but readers will always make the story their own. Both conceptual and empirical research is the retelling of others' stories.

To be authentic, however, the researcher must be able to hear what has been said, through the voices of either research subjects (e.g. the students and teachers we interview) or those who have written and published their accounts. In this way, qualitative or mixed methods research is ultimately about learning: learning from others and helping others to learn. Publication is partly about sharing knowledge through accounts that others will want to read. In essence, the job of a qualitative researcher is to make complex stories accessible and represent a certain truth that enables a contribution to knowledge and the theories and practices of the field. When we use the term 'stories', other research methodologists may see this as a pejorative term or claim research as a more 'serious' academic endeavour, but we argue for the idea of the research narrative as a powerful way of helping ourselves, and others, to make sense of the world. Constructing these narratives relies on systematic and rigorous thinking as well as creativity at every step of the research.

It is important to return to the idea that two different researchers using the same methods to answer the same question are likely to come up with different interpretations and conclusions, unless they have identical ontological and epistemological perspectives. As such, multi-authored narratives are negotiated, require compromise and cannot be relied on to reflect a single shared ontological and epistemological position. Finally, learning to research gives epistemic access to how knowledge is produced in a discipline or field with access coming from an understanding of methodology. All successful researchers have the ability to judge the worth of knowledge claims and contribute original ideas to a field and make a difference. The foundation of this is methodological, and so particular thinking skills are developed while learning the established research processes of the discipline. However, an epistemological status quo should on no account be accepted at face value, and established ways of knowing must themselves be open to critique and open to change.

Bibliography

Bryman, A. & Bell, E. (2003). *Business research methods*. Oxford, UK: Oxford University Press.

Cousin, G. (2010). Repositioning positionality. In M. Savin-Baden & C.H. Major (Eds.), *New approaches to qualitative research: Wisdom and uncertainty* (pp. 9–18). New York, NY/Abingdon, UK: Routledge.

Feyerabend, P. (1975). *Against method*. London, UK: Verso.

Grix, J. (2002). The generic terminology of social research, *Politics*, 22, 3: 175–186.

Harland, T. (2012). Higher education as an open-access discipline, *Higher Education Research and Development*, 31, 5: 703–710.

Harland, T. (2014). Learning about case study to research higher education, *Higher Education Research and Development*, 33, 6: 1113–1122.

Macfarlane, B. (2016). *Freedom to learn: The threat to student academic freedom and why it needs to be reclaimed*. Abingdon, UK: Routledge.

Morrow, W. (2009). *Bounds of democracy: Epistemological access in higher education*. Cape Town, South Africa: HSRC Press.

Polanyi, M. (1958). *Personal knowledge: Towards a post-critical philosophy*. Chicago, IL: University of Chicago Press.

Rushdie, S. (2012). *Joseph Anton: A memoir*. New York, NY: Random House.

Saunders, M., Lewis, P., Thornhill, A. & Wang, C.L. (2009). Analysing quantitative data. In M. Saunders, P. Lewis & A. Thornhill (Eds.), *Research methods for business students* (5th ed). UK: Prentice Hall.

Seale, C. (1999). Quality in qualitative research, *Qualitative Inquiry*, 5, 4: 465–478.

van Manen, M. (1998). *Researching lived experiences: Human science for an action sensitive pedagogy*. London, UK: The Althouse Press.

Wheelahan, L. (2014). Babies and bathwater: Revaluing the role of the academy in knowledge. In P. Gibbs & R. Barnett (Eds.), *Thinking about higher education* (pp. 125–137). Cham, Switzerland: Springer International.

3

QUALITATIVE RESEARCH APPROACHES

Introduction

Study design is an important aspect of planning for any project and the researcher will need to decide which research approach is best to answer the research question. Sometimes the solution is obvious and at other times a question can be addressed using a variety of approaches. In this chapter, an overview is provided of each of the common types of qualitative research approach (in Chapter 4 we address quantitative approaches). These are introductions to the topic and are not meant to provide a comprehensive guide to adopting such an approach. Further readings and key texts are provided at the end of the book. In this chapter we describe the following:

1. Phenomenology
2. Grounded theory
3. Ethnography
4. Narrative inquiry
5. Case study

The case study (the subject of Chapter 6) is addressed briefly at this point as an 'approach', because of its central place in higher education research design. However, nearly all empirical research done in higher education is in case study format, regardless of approach and method. We conclude the chapter with some comments on the politics of adopting a research approach.

Choosing the right approach provides clarity and purpose for a research project, including the role of the researcher, the various stages of the project, the method of data collection, the sampling strategy and the methods for data analysis and interpretation. In order to understand qualitative research approaches, it is helpful to be clear about the key features of qualitative research methodology.

Key features of qualitative research

Qualitative research is exploratory research that is essentially inductive, as ideas and concepts emerge from the data and evidence gathered from an empirical study. These ideas are usually presented in propositional forms. We argue that qualitative research is interpretive because all the data, regardless of which approach is taken, requires interpretation by the researcher or research team. A qualitative research project features the following:

- a central phenomenon;
- broad and general questions;
- data that is context dependent and directly reflects the views of participants;
- documenting personal reflexive accounts;
- being flexible with questions and interpretation;
- making meaning or advocating for groups or individuals;
- adherence to the values of reciprocity and respect of participants;
- analysis that leads to a thick description of data themes; and
- research findings that are subject to different interpretation.

These features will all be present but are handled differently depending on the logic of a particular qualitative research approach. Table 3.1 provides an overview of conventional research approaches grounded in qualitative and interpretative epistemology.

1 Phenomenology

Phenomenology is considered a philosophical approach that focuses on people's subjective experiences and interpretations of the world. As a philosophy, phenomenology is associated with the early work of Edmund Husserl, Martin Heidegger and others. There are schools of phenomenology and different types within those schools. Phenomenology is categorized by what the focus of study is. For example, hermeneutic phenomenology studies the interpretive structure of experience.

As a qualitative research approach, phenomenology involves analysis and understanding of the structures of experiential consciousness, as lived activities and phenomena, and the relationships among people and their socio-cultural milieu. It is concerned with questions aimed at understanding the essences of experiences. It might include research questions such as 'what is the nature of this phenomenon as experienced by the people who live in it?' and 'what might this phenomenon mean to participants?' Individuals comprehend an event through how they feel about, relate to or understand it, and phenomenology aims to capture these experiences. The unit of analysis when using phenomenological analysis is the conscious lived experience. The different types of experiences that can be analyzed using phenomenology include feelings, emotions, perceptions, imagination, thought, desire and action.

TABLE 3.1 Conventional research approaches in higher education

Research approach	Research question	Unit of analysis	Analytic strategy	Research outcome
Phenomenology	What are the lived experiences of an academic developer?	Lived experience (what it *means* to be an academic developer, jobs structures, challenges, opportunities)	Phenomenological reduction; hermeneutic analysis	Description of the essential structure of the day-to-day life of an academic developer
Grounded theory	What is an ideal postgraduate education in the 21st century?	Themes	Constant comparative analysis	Factors that contribute to ideal postgraduate education
Ethnography	How are universities managed in different countries?	Culture	Representation, translation, and textualization of culture	Typology of interpretations, relations and variations in systems and management styles
Narrative inquiry	What are the challenges of being a student?	Stories	Generating, interpreting, and representing students' stories	Narrative accounts of students' challenges, experiences and opportunities
Case study[1]	How can a university become a digital campus?	Case (descriptive, exploratory or explanatory)	Case analysis and comparison	Detailed thematic description relative to unique examples of a digital campus

1 Case study can be understood as a separate approach; however, almost all the work done in the field can be categorized as case study (see Chapter 6).

Central to a phenomenological approach is the principle of *epoché*, which comes from an ancient Greek term and means that the researcher needs to suspend judgement about non-evidential matters, maintain some level of openness and suspend notions about stereotypes. Only in this way can the researcher hope to come near to experience a phenomenon as lived and felt by participants. In this way, phenomenology aims to provide an objective approach to what are normally considered subjective subjects.

Phenomenology, like other qualitative approaches, is concerned with the discovery of new knowledge. In practice, the researcher has to focus on particular parts of a phenomenon and so it is essentially a reductionist approach. However, phenomenologists reject this idea as they see the parts only as a means to understanding the whole phenomenon.

2 Grounded theory

Grounded theory is a research approach that seeks to develop a theory grounded in observations or data that have been systematically gathered and analyzed. It allows the researcher to develop a theoretical account of the general features of a topic. Grounded theory requires a continuous interplay between data collection and analysis, and offers a general description or explanation of a research phenomenon. Grounded theory studies are useful in developing context-based, process-oriented descriptions and explanations of a phenomenon. A study can utilize many forms of data. Most common are interviews but a grounded theory can be constructed from surveys and observations.

In grounded theory research, the theory evolves from an initial engagement with the data with preliminary ideas refined in a series of stages that require both initial coding of ideas and memoing. We understand memoing as a process by which an emergent idea is tested theoretically through interplay between the data and published theory. The researcher keeps track of the analysis with memos which can be kept in a field notebook. Eventually memos are sorted into key themes that form the basis of the research write-up.

3 Ethnography

This research approach is concerned with the study of people, cultures and society. Ethnography is typically interdisciplinary and will draw on research traditions from many fields including sociology, history, anthropology and biology. It is essentially a field-based approach that uses observations, although it may exploit a variety of qualitative and quantitative methods. However, observational methods are its foundation (see Chapter 5). An ethnographic study can involve a whole culture, a single person or even the researcher themselves (auto-ethnography). In auto-ethnography, the researcher engages in systematic self-reflection and writing to explore his or her own experiences and connect these to the wider cultural or societal question. The approach seeks to gather data from the whole system being studied (at whatever level) and often requires the construction of emergent key themes from the data (Thomas, 2006). This analytical approach has much in common with a grounded theory analysis.

4 Narrative inquiry

In its simplest form, narrative inquiry is a method of naturalistic inquiry that allows the researcher to collect the stories of respondents and present these in a narrative style. It is an approach that allows the researcher to collaborate with participants over time or published texts and explore in depth the phenomenon or research question (Clandinin & Connelly, 2000). It typically uses stories, field notes, video and diaries, as well as other artefacts, but also employs more traditional methods of data collection such as interviews. The main principle behind this approach is that narrative is seen as a powerful way of sharing knowledge, both in the 'telling' and in representation. We suggest that when the subject of research is highly complex and not easily studied by more common methods, or is located in participant experiences over a long period of time, the researcher should consider a narrative approach. The challenge in using narrative inquiry is to write an account that has utility and Clough (2002) suggests that it is only useful if it opens up to its audiences a deeper view of life in familiar contexts. This idea seems very pertinent to higher education research in which the researcher is part of the social fabric of the subject. Those who work in higher education are usually very familiar with the situations that they are questioning.

The key arguments for the effectiveness of narrative inquiry is that we live storied lives, talk about ourselves through stories and that stories have great potential for illuminating and helping us understand the infinite complexities of human experiences (Connolly & Clandinin, 1990). In the analysis, the core ideas from the stories and fragments of information that each respondent shares are extracted and the researcher produces a new narrative that a reader can more readily connect with. Of course, each reader will make new realities for themselves but whatever these are, and like all research, the account should have originally been written to both inform professional practices and make a contribution to theory. What the researcher is essentially doing is telling new stories that have been derived from older accounts of experience. These older accounts are the data that are collected through interviews and other methods and then transformed in some way to provide the research outcome (Polkinghorne, 1995).

There is probably no such thing as a 'true' story (Riessman, 1993) and so narratives usually appear as semi-fictional. However, in analyzing data, the researcher can look for 'grand narratives' that have some equivalence to emergent themes in interview-research. Bruner (1996) argued that reading narratives will be neither rational (in terms of determining a truth) nor empirical (in terms of a method for the verification of text), and as such, narrative accounts can be seen as 'unfinished' research. Connelly and Clandinin (1990) recognize a dual function in narrative inquiry in that it tends to have a major impact on the research respondent's learning.

In a study that used this method (see Harland and Pickering, 2011, for an illustration of narrative inquiry) the narratives presented enabled the reader to feel empathy with the characters and situations described (Bolton, 2006). It was argued that this is something often lacking in traditional research forms and that empathy helps the reader understand the person behind the story. These stories are a different route to understanding the world and there is no doubt that narrative inquiry has now achieved qualified acceptance as a research method by some in the broader academic community. However, it is not without its critics, and it still remains on the fringes of mainstream educational research. Like all research approaches, it has its strengths and limitations. It is also hard to distinguish 'pure' narrative inquiry from the broad range of narrative analysis types that have emerged since Connolly and Clandinin's (1990) seminal work, and narrative has become embedded in other forms of qualitative study (Caine, Estefan & Clandinin, 2013). We do not regard this co-opting of narrative inquiry as problematic because it is quite a challenge to conduct a pure study and publish it. Embedding narrative in a variety of ways in mainstream qualitative research representations should be considered while the researcher should never lose sight that all research should tell a story.

5 Case study

Qualitative research generally only produces data on the case being studied and it does this regardless of approach or method. In other words, qualitative research is contextual. However, case study has been described both as an approach and as a method. Despite this, it is hard to define and distinguish from other approaches because it can include multiple approaches and methods and also mix qualitative and quantitative approaches. Case studies in higher education are typically quite small but are always unique to the context in which the research has been conducted. In this sense, all empirical research in higher education can be framed as a single case (Chapter 6). The ability to generalize from a case study comes only through the power and worth of the ideas produced, and how these contributions are seen more broadly and the impact they make in the higher education community.

Conclusion

Research design is an important part of the research process because it provides a clear structure and direction for researchers to undertake to produce useful research outcomes. There are many approaches to various types of research methodologies; it is therefore important that the researcher decides on which research approach is best to answer the research question they are interested in pursuing. In this chapter, we have provided common approaches used in qualitative research. Each approach presented in the chapter is underpinned by a particular set of assumptions and heuristics that are critical for undertaking data collection, analysis and reporting of research outcomes. Table 3.1 provides a summary of each approach, the nature of the question associated with it, data analysis strategy, and the unit of analysis commonly used. For a more detailed elaboration on each of the approaches presented in this chapter, we encourage readers to consult with the list of bibliographical references provided at the end of the book.

Bibliography

Bolton, G. (2006). Narrative writing: Reflective enquiry into professional practice, *Education Action Research*, 14, 2: 203–218.

Bruner, J. (1996). *The culture of education.* Cambridge, MA: Harvard University Press.

Caine, V., Estefan, A. & Clandinin, D.J. (2013). A return to methodological commitment: Reflections on narrative inquiry, *Scandinavian Journal of Educational Research*, 57, 6: 574–586.

Clandinin, D.J. & Connelly, F.M. (2000). *Narrative inquiry: Experience and story in qualitative research.* San Francisco, CA: Jossey-Bass Publishers.

Clough, P. (2002). *Narratives and fictions in educational research.* Buckingham, UK: Open University Press.

Connolly, F.M. & Clandinin, D.J. (1990). Stories of experience and narrative inquiry, *Educational Researcher*, 19, 5: 2–14.

Harland, T. & Pickering, N. (2011). *Values in higher education teaching.* London, UK: Routledge.

Polkinghorne, D.E. (1995). Narrative configuration in qualitative analysis, *International Journal of Qualitative Studies in Education*, 8, 1: 5–23.

Riessman, C.K. (1993). *Narrative analysis* (Qualitative Methods Series 30). London, UK: Sage Publications.

Thomas, D.R. (2006). A general inductive approach for analyzing qualitative evaluation data, *American Journal of Evaluation*, 27, 2: 237–246.

4
SURVEYS AND OTHER QUANTITATIVE APPROACHES

Introduction

This chapter has been included for researchers considering survey work or other quantitative methods. We provide some of the underlying principles of the quantitative approach and a short guide to statistical analysis. For those who have a qualitative background, we would recommend getting to know a statistician with experience in social research and bringing his or her expertise into a research team. Such a partnership needs to form early in the design process and preferably when decisions about the research question are being made. Bringing in a statistician near the end of a study to help with the final statistical analysis typically results in a situation where the researcher or research team find they have made mistakes that could have been avoided. We have witnessed situations where projects have to be salvaged in some creative way, usually resulting in compromises that are less than ideal.

What this chapter should give to those with a qualitative background is some knowledge of the principles and language of the quantitative research approach, and confidence to talk to and understand a statistician or read a statistics textbook. Some of the ideas in the chapter may feel like a refresher for those with quantitative experience, but we also provide specific ideas about survey and experimental approaches used in the study of higher education, and these will be new to those without this knowledge.

Quantitative approaches in higher education research are based largely on the idea that educational outcomes can be measured and quantified in some way which reflects a particular ontology and epistemology (Chapter 2). These approaches are concerned with expressing study outcomes in some numerical form. Researchers employ quantitative approaches to discover relationships among variables and so any study must isolate specific variables and their operations within the research context.

It is important to know that statistical domains in quantitative research can be classified into sample statistics (descriptive statistics) and population statistics and parameters (inferential statistics). Descriptive statistics describe the basic features of the data gathered, including the distribution or location of averages within a given sample and summaries of data that can be presented in the form of graphs, charts and tables. When quantitative researchers want to test a specific hypothesis and infer population characteristics from a sample analysis, inferential statistics are used. Inferential statistics depend on the theory of probability and the general goal is to estimate the differences between a sample and a population. In other words, when measurements are made in a small part of a population, is it reasonable to infer that the outcomes will apply to the whole population?

Higher education researchers do not always directly measure an educational phenomenon, but rather its characteristic attributes, based on how a research respondent has experienced, interpreted or understood the phenomenon. Numbers in quantitative approaches are then used to represent both observable phenomena (e.g. count data) and unobservable characteristics (e.g. how someone feels). In quantitative research, the researcher needs to be clear about how the variables he or she measures differ because this affects data interpretation and the type of statistical analysis that is appropriate. Understanding variables depends on a concept called 'measurement scale' and in the most common and basic typology there are four scales. These are nominal, ordinal, interval and ratio (see Table 4.1).

Nominal scales are usually used to measure categories or group properties. Numbers assigned are simply identifiers and cannot be manipulated statistically. For example, arbitrary numbers can be assigned to differentiate one country's educational system from another, such as Canada = 1; New Zealand = 2; UK = 3.

Ordinal scales are applied when attributes of a phenomenon can be ranked in a certain order. These are commonly seen in survey approaches. For example, we can rank educational background according to some known hierarchy such as undergraduate student = 1; postgraduate diploma student = 2; master's degree student = 3; PhD student = 4. Although it is implied that PhD is higher than master's training, this scheme does not explicitly tell us the numerical distance between a PhD and a master's. A typical four-category rating scale used in surveys with strongly

TABLE 4.1 Measurement scale and interpretation

Type of scale	Interpretation
Nominal	(Categorical) attributes are named
Ordinal	Attributes can be ordered
Interval	Distance is meaningful
Ratio	Absolute zero

agree (1), mostly agree (2), mostly disagree (3) and strongly disagree (4) is ordinal. Like all ordinal scales, the distance between each attribute is not meaningful. In other words, the difference between 1 and 2 on the scale may not be the same as between 2 and 3.

Interval scales do allow for the degree of difference but not the ratio. In grading students' work, the distance between 30% and 40% is the same as the distance from 70% to 80%. However, the ratio is not the same and a grade of 80% is not twice that of 40%.

Ratio scales have measurements with an absolute zero and allow for both difference and ratio. Examples include such things as mass, weight and length. Two centimetres is half of four centimetres. Ten degrees Celsius is twice that of five degrees Celsius.

These measurement basics are essential for designing surveys and using questionnaire methods because they help the researcher understand the claims that can be made relative to the design process, while providing a guide to an appropriate statistical analysis where this is sought.

1 Survey approaches

Surveys are a common approach to answering certain types of question in higher education studies. Surveys aim to provide a comprehensive, representative summary of specific characteristics, beliefs, attitudes, opinions or behavioural patterns of a population. They are used to study both social systems and specific phenomena in the field. This work is always conducted in response to an overarching a priori research question and generally consists of a series of specific qualitative questions that are each matched by a quantitative ordinal scale. Surveys are attractive to the novice, partly because they are presumed to be easier to construct and administer than conducting interviews or other qualitative techniques. There is no doubt, however, that they are very effective for certain types of question and study design. In addition, they are used for 'triangulation' – the collection of multiple sources of evidence in mixed methods research to understand a complex phenomenon – and for adding extra data and depth to any qualitative study. Surveys can also be used in a sequential manner in mixed methods research. For example, a phenomenon might be explored in a series of in-depth interviews until the data are saturated (the researcher learns nothing more by increasing the interview sample size). Analysis of the interview responses then allows the researcher to construct a much more precise and relevant survey than he or she might otherwise have been able to do. This survey is then administered to a larger sample (i.e. more than the interview sample) of the whole population.

If the intention of a study is to generalize to the population from which the samples have been drawn, survey implementation must adhere to a set of theoretical rules to allow certain claims to be made based on probability statistics or through data modelling. In all cases, implementation of a survey requires some knowledge of statistics because there will typically be a two-step process of preliminary or initial data analysis, and then, and only when required, a more sophisticated in-depth analysis. Even when there are no plans to generalize the findings from the sample to the population, summary or 'descriptive' statistics from the initial data analysis are essential. These allow the researcher to discern, for example, averages, general patterns and possible size effects. Summary statistics can also be used to construct graphs and scatter plots showing the dependent and independent variables. This step of visual representation gives the researcher more of a feel for how to interpret the data and study. We next provide an overview of sampling theory and sampling techniques. A brief account is provided on how to choose the correct procedure for hypothesis testing, of which we will say more below.

Sampling

Research outcomes and generalizations are only as good as the sample that generated the data. Sampling is a key part of both qualitative and quantitative approaches. It is a procedure for recruiting participants, subjects or other forms of data to a study because researchers nearly always study a sample of the whole population. Sampling strategy needs to take into account the characteristics and distribution of the population. The strategy is very important in quantitative research, and in particular for surveys, when outcomes and claims are based on statistical analyses. In a survey, the researcher decides on how many people will need to be included, what individual characteristics of participants are likely to influence responses to questions (random error) and the experimental conditions that might affect the overall quality of data (systematic error). In reality, we find that many researchers do not take into account the theoretical constructs of sampling but simply go through a set of logical and practical steps to design a survey:

1. Decide on obtaining a sample.
2. Determine the sample size.
3. Randomly draw a sample of acceptable size from the population.
4. Decide on the statistic of interest for that sample.
5. Use a theoretical distribution to identify the differences between the sample, characteristics and the theoretical properties of the population.

Recruiting participants to a study requires the researcher to define a population of interest, specify a sampling frame (or a set of items or events) and calculate the possible sample size. A sampling frame is a list or procedure defining the study population from which a sample will be drawn. For example, it could be a list of all undergraduate students at a university. There are two categories of sampling techniques used to recruit participants. These are non-probability and probability sampling techniques (see Figure 4.1).

48 Surveys and other quantitative approaches

```
Non-probability sampling ─┐                    ┌─ Probability sampling
                          │                    │
        Convenience ──────┤                    ├── Simple random
                          │                    │
        Purposive ────────┼── Sampling techniques ──┼── Stratified random
                          │                    │
        Quota ────────────┤                    ├── Cluster random
                          │                    │
        Snowball ─────────┘                    └── Multistage
```

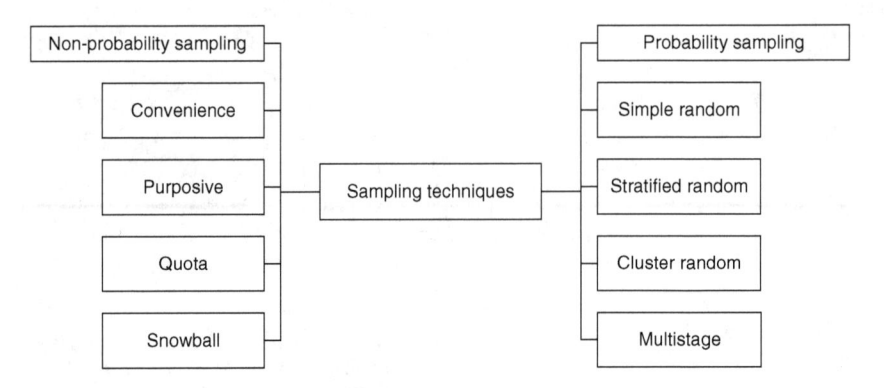

FIGURE 4.1 Categories of sampling techniques

Non-probability sampling

Non-probability (non-random) samples are broadly used in qualitative research approaches but also in quantitative research, in pilot studies and for developing hypotheses for future research. These techniques tend to focus on recruiting volunteers or participants who happen to be present at the time of the study. However, non-probability sampling techniques are limited, because samples do not represent the population from which they are drawn. Common types of non-probability samples include convenience, purposive, quota and snowball.

Convenience sampling

Convenience sampling is also referred to as 'accidental' or 'people-in-the-street' sampling. Randomness can still be applied when the researcher selects participants that are close at hand or easy to reach. For example, the researcher decides whom to approach when interviewing students who happen to be on campus on a Friday. The outcomes of research done in this way cannot be generalized beyond the context in which data were generated.

Purposive sampling

Here samples are selected with a particular purpose in mind. For example, researchers interested in postgraduate students' learning in humanities subjects will only select appropriate respondents who fit this criteria. A distinctive element of this technique is the absolute exclusion and inclusion criterion.

Quota sampling

The researcher constructs quotas from the population of interest but selection is non-random; for example, a fixed number of international postgraduate students with half from North America and half from Africa. There are two ways to draw quota samples; either proportionally or non-proportionally. The researchers calculate equal proportions of individuals on known characteristics or a quota that is independent of population characteristics.

Snowball sampling

Snowball sampling is where a researcher surveys (or interviews) a participant and asks if they could suggest someone else who might be willing or appropriate for the study. This technique is usually applied in a situation where there might be some challenges in getting participants.

Probability sampling

Sampling procedures based on probability theory entail that every unit of the population of interest must be identified. Sampling employs randomization in the selection of individuals from a given population. The key benefit of this technique compared to non-probability sampling is that the researcher can work out a mechanism to ensure that the sample chosen is representative of the population and there is an assumption that all individual members of a population have a chance of being selected. Probability driven sampling types include simple random sampling, stratified random sampling, cluster sampling and multistage sampling.

Simple random sampling

The easiest form is a simple random sample, most common in experimental research because it provides equal chance of inclusion of all participants in the population (Moore & McCabe, 2006). Sample sizes need to be large or representative.

Stratified random sampling

Sometimes referred to as segment or quota random sampling. Samples are taken from a representative strata or segment of the population. Stratification can be more cost-effective than simple random sampling.

Cluster sampling

This type is primarily based on geographical areas or 'clusters' that can be seen as being representative of the whole population. Cluster sampling views the units in a population not only as being members of the total population but as members of naturally-occurring clusters within the population. For example, university students are members of a class, a course and a degree programme.

Multistage sampling

Multistage sampling is a combination of several sampling techniques, aimed at creating a more efficient and effective strategy than a single sampling technique.

Sample size and response rate

In both quantitative and qualitative research understanding sample size is necessary because it enables the researcher to carefully choose the appropriate number of observations or replicates to include in a study. For qualitative research (e.g. how many interviews), this issue is addressed in Chapter 5. For survey work, other quantitative methods and any empirical study in which the goal is to make inferences about a population from a sample, the sample size is crucial. Too small and there will be difficulty in generalizing to the population. Too big and the researcher will have wasted time and money unnecessarily. The second question concerns response rate. In other words, how many surveys are sent out and how many are returned. Key texts that provide a full treatment of sample size calculation are given in the further reading section at the end of the book.

Sample size

The calculation of the sample size depends on the purpose of the study, the research questions and the characteristics of the population. For instance, a larger sample size is usually required to study a heterogeneous population compared to a homogenous one. Sample size also depends on the desired level of statistical confidence required. Many researchers take a pragmatic approach and suggest a minimum of 30 participants per variable. However, we suggest that in higher educational research, and in some observational studies, this number should be quadrupled or a default minimum of 100 cases or participants used to achieve a reasonable effect size. The large sample size is usually required because social and educational phenomena are dynamic entities with multiple interpretations.

Response rate

Response rate is a factor that can influence the generalization of results to the population from which a sample is drawn. A response rate in survey research is calculated as the total number of people who answered the survey, divided by the number of individuals desired in the sample. The higher the response rate, the smaller the sampling error. When we get a small sampling error, then our sample is more likely to resemble the characteristics of the population, meaning that more confidence can be placed on general statements about the population. If, for example, we want to know how postgraduate students value learning research methodology, we can survey them all by drawing on a sample. If an online survey went to 1,000 students who made up the whole population, and only 20 respondents replied, what we can learn from this 2% of the population might not tell us how the rest of the students felt. There are many different views on what constitutes an acceptable response rate. As a rule of thumb, a response rate of between 10% and 100% should be sought. For suggested references on sample size and response rates, refer to the further reading section at the end of the book.

2 Experimental approaches

Across society, the scientific experiment is highly valued as a source of factual knowledge that can be relied on as 'true' in some way, and there is an embedded or instinctive understanding of the power and certainty that comes from being able to explain cause and effect with a high degree of certainty. There is no field of knowledge that has not at least flirted with the idea of research experiments, and higher education is no exception. However, experimental work in higher education is rare.

Essentially experiments are conducted in a manner in which the researcher imposes control over the study procedure, essentially by manipulating certain variables to observe changes in an outcome variable. Experimental research designs in higher education resemble the logic, principles and techniques used in the natural sciences, where researchers frame a research problem, develop a question and form hypotheses. At the conclusion of the research, this hypothesis is either accepted or rejected. Unlike the natural sciences, in which experiments are typically untaken in the laboratory or controlled in the field, in higher education, experiments tend to take place in naturalistic settings such as the classroom.

Experimental work is always concerned with the analysis of cause-and-effect relationships and understanding this concept is central to any experimental design. There are three necessary and sufficient conditions for establishing cause and effect and these are temporal precedence, covariation and no plausible alternative explanation:

1. Temporal precedence requires that cause occurs before effect. For example, students' test grades improve after the teacher has implemented a new educational programme.
2. Covariation is a condition where the research controls the influence of all other variables on the dependent variable (the variable being tested). This removes confounding variables. Covariation assumes that a relationship must exist before one can claim there is a causal relationship in a study. For example, if X is present then Y is present, and so if X is absent then Y is absent. In other words, if the teacher did not implement the new teaching programme, then student test scores would not have improved.
3. No plausible alternative explanation seeks to check if a relationship is caused by some unknown or missing variable. The researcher questions all plausible alternative explanations that might be able to explain the data. To achieve true causality, the researcher must show that it was the new teaching programme that was responsible for students' higher test grades. However, if other factors are responsible for students scoring high grades, then the researcher cannot be confident that the presumed cause–effect relationship is correct. These factors need to be identified and controlled in future studies.

A well-planned and well-executed experiment with good controls is likely to have high internal validity, but there are limitations in contemporary educational settings for the use of such approaches. When dealing with either teachers or learners in genuine and authentic practice situations where the intervention is to be made, there are ethical considerations to take into account. For example, there may be negative consequences for some participants, especially when, for instance, students in a control group are penalized in some way. Of course, 'consequences' will depend on the magnitude and gravity of the situation, but experimental work has a poor history in some instances. In addition, teachers are in a position of unequal power over students and if the teacher is the researcher, or a research collaborator, then care must be taken if they also take part and become an experimental subject or variable.

Typically educational experiments manipulate at least one dependent variable. For example, the researcher divides subjects into two groups. Each is treated equally except that one group receives a different version of the treatment (experimental group). The other group acts as a control. The control group must, apart from the variable being studied, experience the same conditions as the treatment group. Experiments can also be referred to as randomized controlled trials (RCT) typical of clinical research, and despite their limitations, these are considered as the most rigorous ways of determining whether a cause–effect relation exists between treatment and outcome.

With respect to higher education study, we suggest that rigorous experimental work may produce reliable and valid conclusions around cause and effect, but the outcomes and claims can be quite superficial and so only make a small contribution to knowledge in higher education. This is partly related to the fact that only some types of question are genuinely suitable for experimentation, and also because most teaching and learning involves unique individuals placed in complex social situations that are virtually impossible to control in the same way that scientific experiments can be controlled in the laboratory. However, it must also be noted that in some science subjects, particularly in field experiments, it may not be possible to control all variables and this does not prevent the work from going ahead. The results are still examined statistically but claims are based on the most likely or best explanation of cause and effect. This type of work may fall into the category of quasi-experiments.

Quasi-experimental designs

The term 'quasi-experiment' means to resemble a true experiment (Campbell & Stanley, 2015). Quasi-experiments are referred to as natural experiments because variables in the treatment are beyond the control of the experimenter. For example, research subjects, such as students, already differ in some original dimensions, such as age, ethnicity, gender and so on. A quasi-experiment is a research design that has some but not all of the characteristics of a true experiment, but lacks randomization. Instead of randomization, a matching strategy is used. For example, a researcher studying the effectiveness of teaching on learning in a class would choose two groups with matching characteristics. The common types are non-equivalent groups designs, pre- and post-test, and interrupted time-series designs (Campbell & Stanley, 2015).

Quasi-experimental research is more common than true experiments in the study of higher education. This type of study has weak explanatory power compared to true experiments or randomized control trials and will not meet the conditions for proving cause and effect. However, it can detect associations between the intervention and an outcome, without ruling out the possibility that an association was caused by confounding factors.

3 Statistical decision making

We include this brief section to help the new quantitative researcher do some preliminary decision making before they undertake a statistical analysis (Figure 4.2). For those new to this field, we repeat our advice to collaborate with a statistician. Broadly, tests can be grouped into parametric and non-parametric. The parametric statistical models are based on the following assumptions:

- The observations must be independent.
- The observations must be drawn from normally distributed populations.
- The populations must have the same variances.
- The populations must have the same standard deviations.
- Data need to be continuous.

If assumptions for parametric tests cannot be met, then non-parametric tests are most appropriate. However, non-parametric statistics are less powerful (i.e. they are more likely not to find a difference that is there). The family of non-parametric models is based on the following assumptions:

- The distribution does not follow the principles of normality ('bell curve').
- The study uses a nominal or interval level of measurement.
- There is less probability of rejecting the null hypothesis.
- If a test shows a significant difference, strong conclusions can be made.

Conclusion

Quantitative approaches enable descriptions of behaviours and processes that are not directly observable and these unlock higher education research to allow both survey work and experimentation. Working with quantitative approaches requires the formulation of specific questions and testing a hypothesis. It involves carrying out a systematic empirical investigation of a phenomenon and requires a level of skill in numerical analysis and measurement. Research results are typically presented through statistics, tables and graphs.

Quantitative research in higher education largely draws on procedures and techniques from the scientific method. Studies must be empirical and claims based on

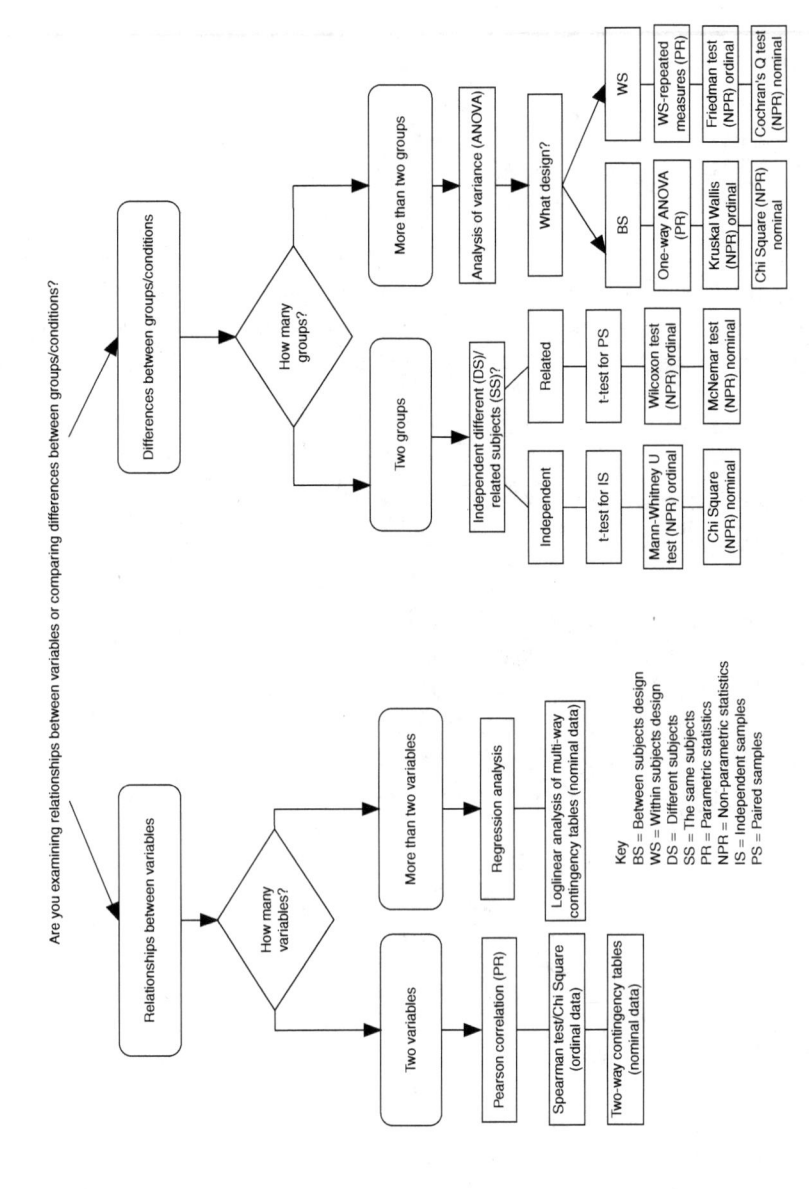

FIGURE 4.2 Decision diagram for choosing a statistical test

evidence. In science, the word 'empirical' refers to the use of a working hypothesis that can be tested using observation and experiment; however, qualitative techniques also claim to be empirical when a research question or hypothesis is tested and data are gathered. Quantitative work is characterized by manipulation, randomization, generalizability to a population, and replicability. Finally, although experiments are rare, surveys and survey instruments are widely used in higher education study and these will be addressed further in the next chapter.

Bibliography

Campbell, D.T. & Stanley, J.C. (2015). *Experimental and quasi-experimental designs for research.* Boston, MA: Houghton Mifflin.

Moore, D.S. & McCabe, G.P. (2006). *Introduction to the practice of statistics* (5th ed). New York, NY: Freeman.

5
RESEARCH METHODS

Introduction

In this chapter, we present five main methods of data collection that are common in higher education research and discuss strategies for employing these and maximizing the quality of data. In particular, we examine the methods used in qualitative approaches and quantitative surveys, although most methods can also be used in either approaches, or in mixed methods research. The chapter examines:

1. Interviews
2. Focus groups
3. Questionnaires
4. Observational methods
5. Video and interpersonal process recall (IPR)

1 Interviews

Interviews are one of the most common methods for data collection in higher education research and provide an incredibly rich source of data when done well. Interviews require a questioning strategy, listening carefully to participants (informants), and creating opportunities for informants to express their thoughts and views freely. What informants say is typically recorded in a digital format and later transcribed. However, responses can be documented during the interview and we would always recommend that field notes be taken as long as the writing process does not interfere with the interview itself. Sometimes participants get anxious or curious when the interviewer starts to write a note in response to a comment. In addition, it can be quite a challenge for the interviewer to write, listen and prepare his or her next response.

We always approach an interview with the idea that we are seeking the co-creation of knowledge with informants through a process of mutual discovery and the testing of ideas and theories. In all cases, there should be a pre-interview briefing in which the researcher reminds the participant about the project, the ethical considerations, how the interview will proceed and that he or she can stop the interview at any point they feel uncomfortable. However, we know that we are in a position of unequal power and this situation needs careful management. It requires putting participants at ease around the process and showing that their contribution is valued while guaranteeing anonymity when appropriate. The researcher can enact a set of values through interactions that are based on careful listening, showing respect for the responses made and not dominating the discussion. However, interviews also require careful balance because the interviewer may need to be critical and probe for deeper or more complete answers. In these contexts, it is a question of judging how far to 'push' respondents. In our experience, the best interviews take place when a level of rapport is developed with the respondent that is based largely on values of trust and respect.

To obtain valid data, it is best to avoid asking leading questions or modifying informants' views about a phenomenon. As such, interview questions are usually non-directive and enable informants to tell their stories, anecdotes and even jokes. Interviews usually take three forms. These are structured, semi-structured and open. In the example given in Table 5.1, the subject of the research is the link between research and teaching, which is an important and current topic of interest in higher education. We have tested the three interview types in Table 5.1 and trials show that the responses and the data obtained are very different for each method.

For the structured interview, the interviewer simply asks each question in turn and the respondent provides an answer. The advantages of this are that the questions are set out in advance, all respondents provide the same set of answers, and this allows for some count data to be used in analysis. When the respondent is articulate and has much to contribute, the interviewer simply listens and perhaps encourages with body language or the technique called 'wait time'. For wait time, the interviewer does not immediately go on to the next question but pauses for a short while (typically a few seconds). The respondent tends to think there is more to be said and may carefully reflect on ideas and add more. This technique must be used cautiously and appropriately as it can create the feeling of an abnormal conversation with unnatural pauses. The risk with the structured interview is that a respondent may give a series of short or superficial answers and so make a minimal contribution to the dataset.

Both semi-structured and unstructured forms of the interview provide the opportunity for both parties to explore questions and answers and develop new conversations around emergent ideas. Either party may return to an earlier question in the interview if something new occurs to them. In the semi-structured form, we always bring a set of possible topics (based on past theory, answer prediction and the research direction) that can be brought in to the interview if necessary. We prefer

TABLE 5.1 Three types of interviews commonly used in higher education research

'Exploring the link between research and teaching in undergraduate courses'

Structured interview	Semi-structured interview	Open interview
1 What do you see as the main benefits of research-led teaching?	1 How do you see the link between research and teaching? [individual level, course level, programme level, department]	1 How do you see the link between research and teaching?
2 How do you draw on research when you are designing a course?		
3 Do your students carry out research projects during their degree? If so, please describe when this happens and how it is done.	2 What do you see as the main benefits of research-led teaching? [difference between university teaching and polytechnic, government policy; for students, for teachers, for the university]	
4 Do you teach a course in research methods? If so, when and how is this done?		
5 How are undergraduate students involved in departmental research activities?	3 How could this link be improved? [current barriers, mass higher education, accountability, education of researchers/teachers to see the link]	
6 How do colleagues in your department link research and teaching?		
7 Could you describe how institutional policies have helped you link research and teaching?		
8 What helps you link research and teaching?		
9 What hinders you linking research and teaching?		
10 Is there anything else you would like to add?		

the respondent to guide us in the conversation and if the follow-up questions have been predicted correctly, most will be addressed from respondent leads.

For the completely unstructured interview there is a large 'unknown' component in how the interview will proceed as little is planned in advance. However, with experience, these types of interview can be the most enlightening of all, and lead to discoveries and new questions that might even be outside the original study

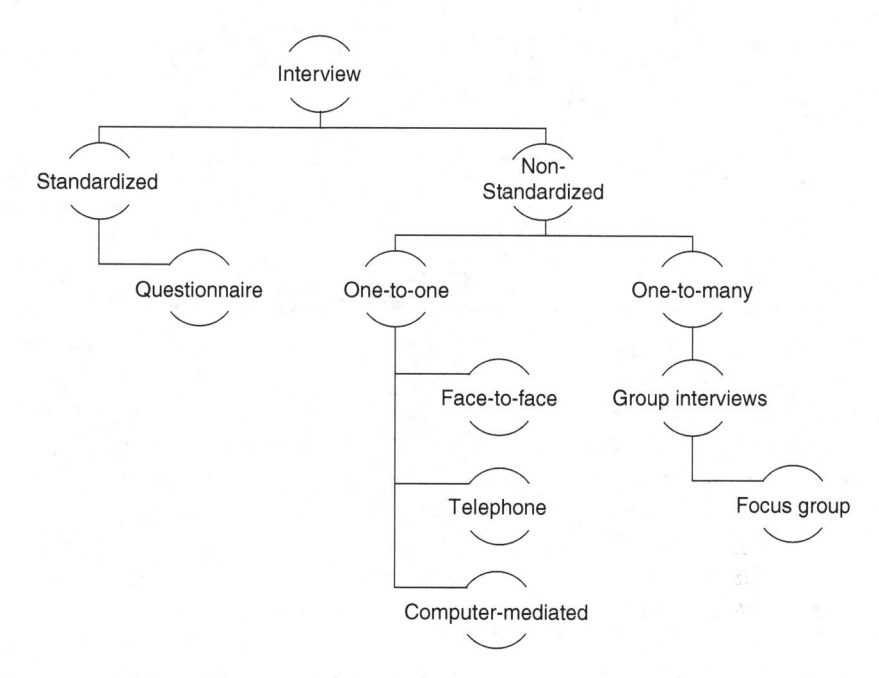

FIGURE 5.1 Interview context framework

parameters but are powerful enough to change the direction of the study itself. In our opinion, these are the most difficult to learn how to do well, but when a level of expertise is gained, they are the most rewarding. The novice can start out using a structured interview, graduate to a semi-structured format and then to unstructured as expertise is gained in the craft. As a safety net, when learning to use a completely unstructured technique, the probe questions listed in Section 5 below may be worthwhile bringing to the interview and using when the interview stalls. When the unstructured interview is mastered, the interviewer will find that they are conducting part of the data analysis during the interview and may base the next line of questioning on some preliminary conclusions.

Interviews take place in different ways, contexts and settings and we present an interview context framework (ICF) that shows the choices for method (Figure 5.1).

Regardless of method, researchers must acknowledge that the quality of any data collected reflects the subjective experiences of participants. Informants are expected to express themselves in the way they speak and construct reality. Moreover, the quality of the interviewing techniques and the experience of the interviewer play a major part.

How many interviews should I do?

A common question is, how many people should be interviewed? This depends firstly on the research question and the answer can range from one to infinity. In addition, it may not be possible to know this figure in advance. For example, a very complex or controversial phenomenon might require a large number of participants. One way of approaching this is to continue interviewing until data are saturated (see Chapter 8). In other words, as more interviews are added, nothing new is learned. We generally feel we have reached saturation when the final two or three interviews yield nothing more, but there is no hard and fast rule about this. It seems to work for us.

On the other hand, we often have constraints on what we can and cannot do. For example, we may not have the finances or time to continue until saturation or may be required to stipulate the number of interviews before the project starts. In these cases, we carry out as many as we can with respect to how we see the phenomenon we are interested in. This task is subjective but experience has shown that between 10 and 20 interviews with an exploratory format (semi-structured or unstructured) suffice, but we would like to be at the upper end of this rough figure for structured interviews. Of course, making such decisions about numbers in this way opens us to criticism, but the reality is that it has 'worked' for us (e.g. Jeyaraj & Harland, 2014) and all our master's and PhD students. If there is any uncertainty about following this advice, then the new researcher can look at the methods sections of relevant published empirical studies and see how many interviews others have needed to do before they have something of worth to say and contribute.

2 Focus groups

Focus groups are a type of group interview. The goal is to facilitate a group discussion on a topic in a manner that enables a range of responses to questions. There are several key aspects that need to be considered.

First, a focus group should never be treated as a cost-effective way of interviewing several people at once. New ideas need to be created through group member interaction and this is what makes focus group work different to interviews and be powerful as a research method. When it works well, an exchange of views prompts new thoughts or brings tacit knowledge to the fore. Individuals can listen to others' ideas and then re-evaluate what they have contributed or what they are presently thinking. The context allows group members to engage and reflect deeply and critically on their experiences in relation to the research question.

Focus groups can also provide an opportunity to build consensus on a topic or a collective knowledge base that can be used to generate a hypothesis for further research questions. They are often used in pilot studies in higher education to gauge the range of possible views and responses and so help in the design of the main research project. Of course, they can be triangulated with other methods of data collection such as questionnaires.

The main challenge of focus group work is facilitating the group discussion. If not properly moderated, individuals that are more vocal and opinionated can hijack the session and dominate discussion, which can bias outcomes and result in lost opportunities for exploration. It is also important to plan how to handle people who are quiet. To address both these problems, a clear engagement protocol should be shared with participants before the interview. This protocol lays out ground rules with respect to what is expected of individuals.

In addition to this, the focus group facilitator needs a rough plan of questions, similar to the semi-structured interview protocol, and to be prepared to make notes as he or she listens to discussions. It is best to jot down participants' names after they introduce themselves. These last two points are crucial to the art of facilitation, because when several members of a group respond in a turn-taking type of dialogue, discussion can drift away from an important idea. In these circumstances it can take a while before there is new space for the facilitator to ask a question that he or she may have wished to have had clarification on much earlier. If the correct observations and notes have been made during the discussion, the facilitator can then go back to the earlier point and specifically address the person who made it and start discussion again. It is very hard to hold this information in one's head and listen to the discussion.

Where focus groups are limited is in dealing with sensitive or political issues that people might relate to very differently, if at all. Researchers can ask themselves whether they would be happy exploring such an issue in public with either friends or strangers. These types of controversial topics need to be addressed using one-to-one interviews in a more private setting in which anonymity can be guaranteed. If sensitive issues do crop up in a focus group and individuals strongly disagree with each other, the facilitator (or other group member) may have to mediate and resolve any conflict.

As part of the sampling strategy, the researcher needs to decide on who will make up the focus group. Depending on the research question, different attributes could include experience with the topic, age, gender or educational background. Finally, how big should a focus group be? Students and academics that we work with always ask this question, and it is important to consider the ideal number of individuals in a group. There will be many views about this across the academic community but we suggest a minimum of three and a maximum of eight participants is ideal in a 60–90 minute focus group session.

3 Questionnaires

Questionnaires are instruments for collecting quantitative data to measure social, behavioural and educational phenomenon. They usually consist of a set of questions with a choice of answers and may also have a qualitative dimension. There are many types of questionnaires used in higher education research but self-completed or self-reported questionnaires seem to dominate. New researchers tend to think the development of a questionnaire is relatively straightforward, and it is possible to go about the task without much prior knowledge and experience (and have a great measure of success). However, we argue that questionnaires, particularly those aimed at developing a standard instrument to objectively measure an educational phenomenon (e.g. knowledge, skills and attitudes), may require significant knowledge that adheres to the principles of psychometrics, a field with its roots in

Research methods

psychology. These principles ensure that a questionnaire is rigorous, meets the needs of the research and is appropriate to the sample. At this advanced level, consulting with a researcher with expertise in psychometrics (in either measurement theory or statistics) is a good idea.

Designing questionnaires

Several steps are often involved in questionnaire development. The first is to identify the overarching aim of the research and link this to the central question being addressed. Once this is determined, a strategy is required to generate survey question items. While questionnaires typically produce quantitative data, many include questions that elicit more in-depth qualitative information. In such a case, there needs to be consideration of the use of closed and open-ended questions. Regardless of type, question generation should never lose sight of the research objective. Where a questionnaire requires validation and tests for reliability a standardized instrument is encouraged where this is available. However, when working on a new area that has no standardized or validated instrument, we always recommend the generation of a blend of quantitative and qualitative questions. A carefully considered mix can provide both breadth and depth on the issue of interest, and get the most from the responses. Types of questionnaire questions are shown in Table 5.2.

TABLE 5.2 Types of questions in questionnaires

Question types	Characteristics	Example	Response choice
Dichotomous	A dichotomous question has two possible responses	Do you think students should be taught epistemology in postgraduate school?	• Yes • No
Nominal	Nominal questions use numbers as placeholders for responses	Please indicate your occupation.	• 1=Professor • 2=Lecturer • 3=Student
Ordinal	Ordinal questions direct respondents to rank their responses	Rank these languages in order of your preference to learn, where 1 is the first preferred choice and 4 is the least preferred choice.	1. French 2. Dutch 3. Norwegian 4. Chinese
Interval	Interval is also known as a Likert response scale. Likert responses can be arranged on a bipolar scale of 1–5 (or 1–4 with no neutral position that leads to 'forced choice')	Speaking more than two languages can increase your reasoning capacity.	• Strongly agree • Agree • Neutral • Disagree • Strongly disagree

Each questionnaire should start with a brief but clear explanation of research and include instructions on how the survey should be completed. To help with questionnaire engagement, questions need to follow a logical and sequential order related to the concepts being studied so that respondents can clearly understand each item. It is advisable to present questions that move from the general to the specific, keep sensitive questions to a minimum and avoid confrontation. Question items can be made compulsory, though in our experience, this tends to contribute to poor response rates. So it is important to ensure that respondents are able to skip a question if they want to.

We have observed that new researchers may wish to include everything they can think of in one questionnaire, making it longer than necessary. A useful questionnaire is one that presents only the most important questions and minimizes the less important ones. As a rule of thumb, the shorter the survey and more direct the questions are, the higher the response rate is likely to be. One of the most common mistakes in survey design is to start the questionnaire with large numbers of demographic questions when these have no bearing on the research question and will never be used or presented in any analysis.

All questionnaires should be pre-tested before being sent out and should include the estimated time it takes to complete. This information helps a respondent decide whether or not to participate. Do they want to spend 10 or 40 minutes on a questionnaire? The pre-test or pilot study allows revision of questions before deployment and provides the average time respondents actually spent on the task. The following are some of the common problems when writing survey questions:

- Double-barrelled questions (more than one issue)
- Vague questions
- Double negatives
- Negative questions
- Leading questions
- Premature assumptions/bias
- Insufficient alternatives with forced-choice options
- Answer options which do not fit with the question

In Table 5.3 we provide a list of ideas about question content and questionnaire layout that the survey designer may wish to ask.

4 Observational methods

Observation is part of most data collection methods in higher education research but its systematic use as a method is not reported often. It is much more common in educational psychology. Observational methods are generally used in natural settings and have the aim of gaining a holistic understanding of the phenomenon being studied. Observational methods are usually interpretive and must take into account a series of limitations including full access to the phenomenon being watched and the cultural filters of those carrying out the observation.

TABLE 5.3 Summary of key points for questionnaire design

Content related	Layout related
Is the question necessary/useful?	Is the questionnaire self-explanatory?
Are several questions needed rather than one?	Are the questions visually clear?
Will respondents have the required information?	Are questions logically grouped and sequenced?
Does the question need to be more specific?	Do the questions in the questionnaire have clear response options?
Is the question biased?	Is the structure of questions clear to respondents?
Is the question about sensitive information?	Are there clear directions for answering questions?
Will the question have only one response per respondent?	Overall, is the questionnaire elegant and simple?
Overall, do all questions relate to the primary research goal/hypothesis?	Are questions simple and to the point?
Are questions clear and relevant to the research purposes (e.g. generalize to a population or not)?	Does the questionnaire take the estimated time?

There are two main classes of observation and these have particular methods (see Table 5.4).

TABLE 5.4 Types of observational method

Direct observation	Indirect observation
a) Without intervention	c) Physical data
b) With intervention	d) Document analysis

Direct observation without intervention

This usually occurs in naturalistic settings where those being observed are unaware that research is going on. The sort of data produced is rich and descriptive but has little explanatory power with respect to cause and effect. There are unresolved ethical questions around this form of direct observation, particularly with respect to individual participant consent. Direct observation without intervention is often associated with an ethnographic research approach.

Direct observation with intervention

In higher education research, direct observation with intervention is more commonplace and occurs in situations in which the participants know the researcher is present. Participant observation is the most commonly used form and it can occur in several different contexts. For example, a researcher may sit in a classroom and observe the teacher, either as an independent observer or as a research collaborator in partnership with the teacher. Other examples include manipulation and experiments where, for example, a new teaching technique might be tried out or a new curriculum introduced. The method of interpersonal process recall (IPR) (see Section 5 below) is a type of direct participant observation with intervention. Note that there is an element of this in other research approaches such as focus groups, in which the facilitator writes down observations in a field notebook.

Indirect observation with data analytics

Here the researcher uses physical artefacts and traces to help answer a research question. Digital technologies such as video cameras and sensors have made it much easier to record events. Data can include such things as how many key strokes a student makes on a computer, which programs were accessed and for how long, and how many posts have been made to a discussion. Digital technology, social media and the new fields of learning analytics and big data unlock the potential for new research and new types of research question.

Indirect observation through document analysis

Much information is archived and document analysis can provide a rich source of data and an opportunity for triangulation in mixed methods research. Universities in particular are very good at keeping thorough records and these can include many types including exam results, staff demographic data and policy documents. Increasingly these documents are found in digital form, which makes access and manipulation theoretically easier. No longer does a researcher have to cross the world and visit a distant library. However, these forms of data may not always be freely available and within an institution may be too sensitive to release (e.g. student pass rates, student attrition and staff turnover).

5 Video and interpersonal process recall (IPR)

Interpersonal process recall (IPR) originated in the field of clinical supervision (Kagan et al., 1969) but has become a widespread research technique that can be used whenever careful and deep reflection on an event is required. In its most common form it is a video technique that helps respondents recall specific thoughts and emotions about the event that they have been part of. In this context, it is sometimes called stimulated recall (STR) (Vesterinin, Toom & Patrikainen, 2010) but the principles are the same for both when video is the medium used.

In research on teaching, for example, a class might be video recorded and then afterwards the teacher sits with an 'inquirer' (in our experience the inquirer is usually the researcher) to review the recording. The teacher stops the video at a point of interest (normally related to the research question) and the inquirer then facilitates a conversation designed to encourage the teacher to reflect on the phenomenon or event of interest, but without leading this process. The strength of the

Inquirer's pre-amble

1 We have discussed IPR in relation to your enquiry and have established what my role should be throughout this recall.
2 I want you to re-live as fully as possible the situation in which you will see yourself as a teacher and try to visualize the thoughts you had during that session.
3 Keep focused on your thoughts *during* the session and not on what you may have thought about since.
4 You can stop as often as you like in order to allow time for full exploration and disclosure of your thoughts.
5 My questions are an invitation to you to do some exploring. If you don't wish to answer them or don't feel that they are helpful, then it's fine to pass and move on.

Examples of inquirer leads

1 Why did you stop the video?
2 Is there anything you would like to add at this point?
3 What were you feeling at that time?
4 Why did you do that?
5 Were you having any other thoughts at that point?
6 How did you want that person to perceive you?
7 How would you have usually responded?
8 How would you like to have responded?
9 How do you think he/she would have reacted if you had said that?
10 What do you think the student(s) would have wanted from you?
11 Do you often feel like that?
12 What do you think was the impact of your actions?
13 What would the risk have been in saying/doing that?
14 Did you know what you were going to do next?
15 What do you think the student was feeling?
16 What did you think?
17 Has that ever happened before?

Close

We have come to the end of our recall session. Is there anything you would like to add? [Before the recorder is switched off – if the recall is being recorded.]

FIGURE 5.2 Protocol for interpersonal process recall (IPR)

technique lies in the fact that participants have an opportunity to look again at what occurred and so reflect on experiences that would not normally be accessible (Laurillard, 2002). In addition, and outside of the technique, the video itself can provide an additional source of data for a study. Once the recording is complete and the researcher (inquirer) sits down for the IPR session, there are a series of systematic steps that should be followed (Figure 5.2). Note that the actual IPR session may also be recorded and form a source of data for later analysis.

The pre-amble and the inquirer leads are designed to allow space for the teacher to reflect without being steered or influenced with respect to a particular line of reasoning, or having to respond to the inquirer's agenda. In practice, it is quite a challenge to adopt this neutral position, especially if it is the researcher who takes the role of the inquirer. IPR can also use other recording formats to help recall, such as audio-recordings and written reflections. However, the video technique is powerful and provides an alternative to teacher or classroom observation.

Conclusion

Structured, semi-structured and unstructured interviews remain the dominant method of collecting empirical data in higher education research. These are qualitative, so when a quantitative approach is required, then surveys and survey instruments take over. In between these central methods there are many others and we have made some remarks about focus groups, observational research and IPR. What we are essentially talking about with respect to the term 'method' is 'data collection' and data hardly ever seems to be correlated with, or confined to, a single method. For example, spoken responses in an interview may be very similar to written responses to the same question in a survey, and when employing a single method, it invariably involves other sources of data. In this sense, most methods used in the study of higher education are, in fact, mixed methods and we would encourage this tradition, not least because it usually helps to have more than one data source for both in-depth understanding and triangulation.

Bibliography

Jeyaraj, J.J. & Harland, T. (2014). Transforming teaching and learning in ELT through critical pedagogy: An international study, *Journal of Transformative Education*, 12, 4: 343–355.

Kagan, N., Schauble, P., Resnikoff, A., Danish, S. & Krathwohl, D. (1969). Interpersonal process recall, *The Journal of Nervous and Mental Disease*, 148, 4: 365–374.

Laurillard, D. (2002). *Rethinking university teaching: A conversational framework for the effective use of learning technologies*. New York, NY: Routledge.

Vesterinin, O., Toom, A. & Patrikainen, S. (2010). The stimulated recall method and ICTs in research on the reasoning of teachers, *International Journal of Research Methods in Education*, 33, 2: 183–197.

6
THE SINGLE CASE

Introduction

We work as higher education researchers in academic development and, like most other developers, we both started our university careers in another field before making the switch. We worked in pure science and computer science and the new subject of higher education was unfamiliar territory. Nearly all the published accounts of research that seemed relevant to academic development work were qualitative and did not follow the rules and methods of science. As a consequence, learning about qualitative inquiry became central to our work. Qualitative inquiry remains the dominant research methodology for articles published in the Australasian and European higher education journals (Tight, 2012) and it is this paradigm that we mainly teach to new higher education researchers. Those who enrol in our research methods course are fellow academics from all disciplines, with the majority having little or no experience of the common methods used to study higher education. Our goal has been to support others as they attend to the many challenges new higher education researchers face (Mcfarlane & Grant, 2012).

We also referee potential articles for a number of higher education journals and find that most are below the standards expected (see Chapter 11). Acceptance rates for these journals are not published, but listening to journal editors talk about this issue at conferences suggests that they are very low, certainly for those journals in the top rank. Rates will vary within and between journals and a number of factors impact on whether or not an article is published, including pre-screening by editors and space shortages. However, acceptance rates of about 10% are probably realistic. If this is correct, the high rejection rate must in part reflect inadequate research expertise. As referees, we see many accounts of practice and innovation that have not progressed far enough to make an adequate contribution to knowledge, usually because of a lack of methodological rigour, clear understanding of the standards required and poor design.

TABLE 6.1 Number of case studies published in four higher education journals, 2007–2012

Journal	Editorial location	Case study	Conceptual study	Total number of articles
Higher Education	Europe	344	181	525
Studies in Higher Education	Europe	238	62	300
Teaching in Higher Education	Europe	176	111	287
Higher Education Research & Development	Australasia	146	101	247
Total		904	455	1359

An article is defined as a case study if the research examined a single event (N=1) and described a method and data collection. Conceptual studies analyzed arguments, theories or concepts and did not report research methods and data collection.

All those we work with and most of the papers we read as a referees use a case study approach and this is very common in higher education. Table 6.1 shows the relative proportion of case studies to conceptual studies published in four of the key Australasian and European higher education journals over a five-year period.

Case study consists of empirical inquiries of single cases that are contextually unique (Stake, 1995) and usually address a problem or an intervention of interest to the researcher's professional practice. The work firstly benefits the researcher undertaking the project and then, when new learning and knowledge are applied to practice, it can have utility for others. In higher education, beneficiaries typically include an academic's students and colleagues in course teams. In this context, it has intrinsic value as an activity, but under the right conditions, a case study can also contribute to the theories and practices of higher education. If this can be achieved, inquiries can be published. There are specialist higher education journals (e.g. Table 6.1) and most disciplines also publish educational case studies, such as medical education and accounting education. So research can be more broadly inclusive or discipline-specific (Harland, 2012).

Qualitative research novices find studying the 'subject of one's own teaching' a challenge and there are a few recurring conceptual problems that create a temporary impasse when learning case-study research methods. We call these 'sticking points':

1. What is the potential of case study?
2. What forms of data are acceptable?
3. When does analysis stop?
4. What makes a quality case study?

In relation to these sticking points, the following questions are addressed:

- Would a closer examination of each point contribute to an understanding of higher education methodology?
- Would such an inquiry have utility for those wishing to learn about case study?

1 What is the potential of case study?

Case study has its detractors and it is typically criticized for being specific to the circumstances of individual practice and therefore limited in what it can offer theory. Taken as a whole, most case studies in higher education are qualitative in nature and in such a paradigm there is none of the certainty that the technical-rational view of knowledge seems to bring (Carr & Kemmis, 1986). In case study there is nothing approaching the elegance and simplicity of the scientific method, even when quantitative data are used. The qualitative paradigm consists of inquiry that requires an individual researcher or research team to analyze data that are open to various interpretations, and each inquirer's experience can provide a different understanding. In this sense, the unique circumstances of the case are contingent on the individual.

We are trained scientists and when we do case research in higher education we feel the strong pull of positivist analogues, such as controls, replication, reliability and generalization. We have gradually learned to put such feelings aside and have found that studying one's own social practice requires another form of science and new standards of judgement (Flyvbjerg, 2006). Flyvbjerg explains this difference by contrasting rule-based knowledge with case-based knowledge, with the distinction being that the latter is always context dependent. No two practice contexts are ever genuinely the same and so rules and deterministic models for guiding thinking and action are not that useful. Yet to help understand complex real-life social situations requires either a) experience or b) learning from specific cases. Eisner (1998) suggests that: 'One of the most useful of human abilities is the ability to learn from the experiences of others. We do not need to learn everything first hand' (p. 202). Initial learning from the case then calls for a further process of careful reflection as new ideas are integrated into thinking, changes are made to practice and the consequences of those changes are evaluated.

It is important for the new researcher to recognize that in case study, for the case itself, $N = 1$. Neither the researcher nor reader can truly replicate the study, they can only learn from it. It matters little if the project is about an educational system or a single teacher's experiences; it is still a single case if it is dependent on a specific social context in time and place. Secondly, if the work is published, the researcher will come to realize that what each reader will learn from the case may be different, even if there is a strong conceptual or theoretical message in the work (Sandelowski & Barroso, 2002). It is well understood that learning is not necessarily contingent on teaching or what a writer intends for their reader. From a case we '… learn a little something (maybe a lot, who knows?) about something we are interested in. On the basis of that little something, we construct a complete story of the phenomenon' (Ragin & Becker, 1992, p. 211).

So it is unusual for the outcome of a case study to generalize in the same way that natural science data can, although this is possible (Denzin, 2009). Flyvbjerg (2006) suggests that there is no reason why knowledge from case studies cannot 'enter the collective process of knowledge accumulation in a given field or in society'

(p. 227). This form of knowledge transfer may happen in different ways. There is the 'cumulative' argument, based on the idea that many different cases may be telling us similar things (Stenhouse, 1979; Eisenhardt & Graebner, 2007). However, Eisner (1998) suggests that transfer occurs through a critical process of engagement as ideas appear to the reader; ideas that allow past experiences to be seen in a new light. Cases therefore provide an opportunity for generalization.

Case-study research is seen as better for generating hypotheses rather than theory building (Flyvbjerg, 2006), yet this criticism is conditional to how the term 'theory' is understood. One way of thinking about theory is that it is explanatory and predictive of cause and effect, and as such can direct action. Another comes from a pragmatist perspective that suggests theory and practice may not be distinct spheres and that humans naturally theorize and may act on such theories in practice. In this sense, inquirers constantly generate personal theories as they seek meaning about practices. Such an inductive and experiential process requires an acceptance that the act of reasoning is a form of personal theory building.

Although either type of theory can provide an explanatory structure, it has been argued that personal theory is most important for the practitioner because of its greater potential to guide us (Schön, 1987). For the case researcher who publishes their work, there are challenges in purposefully 'transferring' personal theories because they can lack specificity for the reader. As a general rule, however, the overall theoretical relevance and the quality of an inquiry tends to be enhanced if existing theories (of various types) are carefully integrated in the work, so that the researcher can make a critical contribution to the wider knowledge field through new interpretations of data (Trowler, 2012). Existing theory should be seen as an integral part of the case.

Lastly, case study has the potential to be personally satisfying because there are few conceptual or methodological boundaries to constrain an inquiry and each project, if done well, involves some form of discovery as new knowledge and theory emerge from the case process.

2 Which forms of data are acceptable?

A frequent assumption is that case study is a qualitative method that excludes quantitative data, but various research methods can be used where appropriate (Yin, 1981; 2006). It is not necessary to choose between paradigms and case study may rely on multiple sources of evidence and be practised as multi-method research (Denzin & Lincoln, 1994). A researcher should feel confident to include, for example, quantitative surveys that examine frequencies or numerical institutional data archives, if these help to answer the research question. Although this idea may appear to be of little consequence, it has been a revelation for nearly all the qualitative novices on our research methods course. However, although it may be possible and/or desirable to incorporate quantitative data in qualitative studies, it is not a common practice choice. In Tight's study on discipline and methodology in higher education research, out of 440 recently published articles from 15 leading higher education journals, only 5% adopted a mixed quantitative/qualitative methodology (Tight, 2012).

3 When does analysis stop?

The outcomes of any chosen analytical technique depend on the researcher's intentions, theoretical background knowledge, the way they think, how they see the world and how they understand and value knowledge. To test this assertion, simply collaborate with another researcher and you will experience differences in all these areas. An end point of analysis for one researcher is not necessarily the same for another.

Because analysis depends on what the researcher already understands from their experience and what they read in the published literature, the analytical process is recursive and it typically moves between the data, published articles, the researcher's developing ideas and then back to the data. Borman, LeCompte and Goetz (1986) point out that 'each investigatory, analytical and conceptual decision is contingent both on those that preceded and those that follow' (p. 54). In this iterative sense, analysis gradually becomes more critical. Dewey's proposition that the 'essence of critical thinking is suspended judgment; and the essence of this suspense is inquiry to determine the nature of the problem before attempts at a solution' (Dewey, 1910, p. 74) suggests that analytical conclusions ought to be provisionally held until ideas can be taken no further. Even at this final stage, a conversation with colleagues or reading in a new literature can open up new thoughts.

Analysis starts during research question formulation and stops (temporarily) when the research gets published. It occurs during the literature review, data collection and formal analysis, and in particular when writing up. Novice researchers often spend a great deal of time on reading, coding and re-analyzing transcripts while heavily engaged in a new literature and continually finding new ways of thinking about the data. It seems to become never-ending. Typically a first reading gives most of the key research outcomes and too much fine-grained distillation early on can arrest progress. To help facilitate this task, the time between collecting data and starting to write the research account ought to be as short as possible. This is because disciplined writing is usually the most essential part of the analytical process. The challenge is to ensure that a pragmatic concern for getting the work done does not interfere with the task of developing new insights and claims to knowledge.

There is no genuine endpoint for a case study but when data feel saturated, in the sense that no more learning comes from the formal analysis and writing, then it is time to call a halt and decide if the work is of sufficient quality to publish, or if more work needs to be done. In our capacities as journal referees, we see frequent attempts to publish research that is rather thin on evidence with respect to the claims being made. Researchers seem to stick to their original data collection protocols but in case study, extra data can be gathered at any stage of the analysis because all forms of qualitative inquiry are provisional.

With respect to interpretation, the researcher does not have to represent all data and may select what is genuinely important to write about (Peshkin, 2000; Siggelkow, 2007). Novices tend to summarize rich data with full description (Flyvbjerg, 2006) but this can lead to superficial outcomes. Morse (1995) suggests that it 'is often the infrequent gem that puts the other data into perspective, that becomes the central key to understanding that data and for developing the model' (p. 148). A researcher starts by considering that each respondent provides a unique information-rich case as part of the wider study, and that what we learn from an individual can be more important than representing the full sample. The written report, however, must reflect such a situation and the analysis aligned with the methodology so the reader feels comfortable with the integrity of the claims being made. In other words, be clear about where the knowledge comes from.

4 What makes a quality case study?

Published accounts that only describe practice can be valuable, but generally have less potential than work that engages the wider theories of higher education. Such a distinction, however, is not enough to help the new researcher appreciate what makes a quality case study. Quality case research, like all research, requires imagination (Dewey, 1938) and creativity (Morse, 1995). It must bring the reader as close as possible to the experience being described (Fossey et al., 2002) and provide conceptual insight (Siggelkow, 2007). Eisner (1998) suggests that all qualitative research needs to be believable and to achieve this the account should be coherent and provide both new theory and instrumental utility. We would add that it also has to be believable in the context of the careful use of evidence in supporting claims, and if it is of quality, it should have the potential to create an impact on the field and practice.

It could be argued that once research gets through a peer review process it will have been judged to have most, if not all, of these properties. However, for the new researcher, learning to make such decisions about their own work can be difficult and 'quality' can be subjective at the best of times. Overall, a case study that is published has to make a contribution to knowledge and if the argument is accepted that someone has to learn from this, then learning also needs to influence action (Rodgers, 2002). If this criterion is used as a proxy for success, can the researcher modify their work to achieve such an outcome?

In published work, other case studies are often cited which suggests that researchers find these useful. One of our published case studies was examined closely to see what evidence there was of wider utility. The articles that had cited this work were read to see how the content had been used. At the time of the analysis, there were 45 citations listed by Google Scholar (43 from others and two self-citations). In the majority of the studies, it would have been impossible to have predicted the rationale behind the citation. For example, what was seen as an important finding in the original article was ignored and what was seen as something relatively trivial was referenced. In one paper, the author was credited for developing a well-known educational theory that was not his. There were patchy data that showed the article had been downloaded from the publisher's website 325 times between 2004 and 2005, 395 times between 2007 and 2008, and 235 times in 2009. These numbers at least suggest the subject was of interest over time. Old email correspondence found that five university lecturers (not higher education researchers) had written from different parts of the world about issues in the article. Finally, workshops based on the findings were developed for university colleagues, new research collaborations were started and a PhD student was recruited. Such a crude and sobering evidence-gathering task echoes the sort of processes favoured in quality assurance and accountability exercises, but it was not clear if this data could genuinely reflect quality in the finished article, unless quality is correlated with a narrow metric view of utility. Turning this around, how do we use others' case studies? In a pedagogic sense, case studies teach about the theories of higher education, how these are applied in real situations and then how the process of application generates new thinking and ideas, for both practice and changing research priorities (Stenhouse, 1979; Flyvbjerg 2006). The reader learns from others making sense of their experiences as they inquire into their own work. However, even when the topic is of interest, very little can be learned from descriptive accounts.

Whenever a new research question is formulated, an initial task is to search for relevant case studies and then sift through them, always looking for ideas that are interesting, insightful or new. In addition, it is essential to read theoretical and conceptual accounts that might seem relevant to a phenomenon, but without experiencing these theories and ideas in academic work, or seeing them tested in a case, it is difficult to judge their practical worth. However, this is a reciprocal process in which understanding of a theoretical idea helps to critically judge what has been described in a case. Both are essential, but it is also how theories are developed at each stage of the research that is of importance (see Clegg, 2012).

Case study is a method of learning (Flyvbjerg, 2006) and a great deal of what has influence will find its way into practice and therefore be 'made public'. Although such an observation takes into account a different form of 'making research public', when research is being done for a journal article or book chapter, it drives thinking to a higher standard. A researcher has to commit ideas to paper, write for a particular audience, follow the conventions of theory-use and, most importantly, present the finished account for critique through peer review. Research made public in other ways may not be subject to such robust critical evaluation and is therefore likely to have less impact on the researcher's learning. Writing for publication also allows the study to reach a wider audience and for the researcher to contribute to their field.

A quality case study will not only have something important to say, but also be well structured and clearly written if it is to be read in the first place. Higher education researchers from other disciplines usually disapprove of educational 'jargon'. It could be argued that there are advantages to serving an apprenticeship in the study of higher education and that learning a new language opens up new possibilities for understanding the education world. However, 'plain speaking' and clarity are also necessary, if the research is conducted for a multi-disciplinary audience characterized by different levels of higher education expertise.

Conclusion

Case study, like all research, has to fulfil its purposes and these need to be worked out by the researcher as a guide to aligning the research process with outcomes. While recognizing that purposes are value-driven, the phrase 'dedicated to intelligent action' is a helpful idea for thinking more generally about why research is done in the first place (a similar point was made about education in general by Dewey in 1939, p. 81). To this effect, case research should be educative, and how well it facilitates learning depends on the quality of the work and how it influences change for the better.

In case study, the unexpected should emerge and when it does, there is potential to make a useful contribution to knowledge, theory and practice. A successful study will explain what the reader or listener needs to consider before they contemplate change and it will be seen as critical in the sense that it avoids being dogmatic in its examination of the case and theory. For writer and reader, any interpretations and their significance will nevertheless be conditional and transitory until understanding changes again. Stenhouse (1981) suggests that inquiries of this sort require certain qualities of the researcher that must sit alongside the technical conventions of systematization. These include 'persistence, a skeptical temper of mind sustained by critical principles, a doubt not only about the received and comfortable answers, but also about one's own hypotheses' (p. 103).

TABLE 6.2 Four challenges for learning case study in higher education

Challenge	Be attentive to ...	Be cautious of ...
What is the potential of case study?	... the work providing an opportunity for learning and for influencing wider theories of practice.	... ignoring existing theory and published accounts in the field; positivist analogues.
What forms of data are acceptable?	... the use of multiple forms of evidence, including quantitative sources where relevant.	... adhering to one type of data collection method.
When does analysis stop?	... the idea that analysis is recursive and never truly stops.	... spending too much time on analysis of primary data before starting to write.
What makes a quality case study?	... providing new and relevant insights, theories and knowledge on which others will act.	... writing descriptively or without a critical audience in mind.

There are huge numbers of books and articles written on case-study methods that can guide the researcher, but because each account is often complex or underpinned by unstated assumptions, following a procedure is never straightforward. Those new to case-study research can experience conceptual and practical difficulties in learning methods, but attempting to resolve complex methodological problems before starting a research project is not always helpful. Case study allows a new researcher to learn from experience, as long as they think of the rules and conventions of qualitative research more as 'guidelines'. Eisner (1998) reminds us that we do not have to learn everything first hand and in this chapter we have identified four sticking points that have been important to those we have worked with. These are summarized in Table 6.2.

Bibliography

Borman, K.M., LeCompte, M.D. & Goetz, J.P. (1986). Ethnographic and qualitative research design and why it doesn't work, *American Behavioral Scientist*, 30, 1: 42–57.

Carr, W. & Kemmis, S. (1986). *Becoming critical: Education, knowledge and action research*. London, UK: The Falmer Press.

Clegg, S. (2012). On the problem of theorizing: An insider account of research practice, *Higher Education Research & Development*, 31, 3: 407–418.

Denzin, N.K. (2009). The elephant in the living room: Or extending the conversation about the politics of evidence, *Qualitative Research*, 9, 2: 139–160.

Denzin, N.K. & Lincoln, Y.S. (1994). *Handbook of qualitative research*. Thousand Oaks, CA: Sage Publications.

Dewey, J. (1910). *How we think*. Boston, MA: D.C. Heath Publishers.

Dewey, J. (1938). *Logic: The theory of inquiry*. New York, NY: Henry Holt and Company.

Dewey, J. (1939). *Experience and education*. New York, NY: The MacMillan Company.

Eisenhardt, K.M. & Graebner, M.E. (2007). Theory building from cases: Challenges and opportunities, *Academy of Management Journal*, 50, 1: 25–32.

Eisner, E. (1998). *The enlightened eye: Qualitative inquiry and the enhancement of educational practice*. Upper Saddle River, NJ: Prentice Hall.

Flyvbjerg, B. (2006). Five misunderstandings about case-study research, *Qualitative Inquiry*, 12, 2: 219–245.

Fossey, E., Harvey, C., McDermott, F. & Davidson, L. (2002). Understanding and evaluating qualitative research, *Australian and New Zealand Journal of Psychiatry*, 36: 717–732.

Harland, T. (2012). Higher education as an open-access discipline, *Higher Education Research & Development*, 31, 5: 703–710.

Healey, M. (2012). Promoting the scholarship of academic development: Tensions between institutional needs and individual practices, *International Journal for Academic Development*, 17, 1: 1–3.

Mcfarlane, B. & Grant, B. (2012). The growth of higher education studies: From forerunners to pathtakers, *Higher Education Research & Development*, 31, 5: 621–624.

Morse, J.M. (1995). The significance of saturation, *Qualitative Health Research*, 5, 2: 147–149.

Peshkin, A. (2000). The nature of qualitative inquiry, *Educational Researcher*, 29, 9: 5–9.

Ragin, C.C. & Becker, H.S. (1992). *What is a case? Exploring the foundations of social inquiry*. Cambridge: Cambridge University Press.

Rodgers, C. (2002). Defining reflection: Another look at John Dewey and reflective thinking, *Teachers College Record*, 104, 4: 842–866.

Sandelowski, M. & Barroso, J. (2002). Reading qualitative studies, *International Journal of Qualitative Studies*, 1, 1: 74–108.

Schön, D. (1987). *Educating the reflective practitioner*. San Francisco, CA: Jossey-Bass Publishers.

Siggelkow, N. (2007). Persuasion with case studies, *Academy of Management Journal*, 50, 1: 20–24.

Stake, R.E. (1995). *The art of case study*. Thousand Oaks, CA: Sage.

Stenhouse, L. (1979). Case study in comparative education: Particularity and generalization, *Comparative Education*, 15, 1: 5–10.

Stenhouse, L. (1981). What counts as research? *British Journal of Educational Studies*, 14, 2: 103–114.

Tight, M. (2012). Higher education research, 2000–2010: Changing journal publication patterns, *Higher Education Research & Development*, 31, 5: 723–740.

Trowler, P. (2012). Wicked issues in situating theory in close-up research, *Higher Education Research & Development*, 31, 3: 273–284.

Yin, R.K. (1981). The case study crisis: Some answers, *Administrative Science Quarterly*, 26: 58–65.

Yin, R.K. (2006). Mixed methods research: Are the methods genuinely integrated or merely parallel? *Research in the Schools*, 13, 1: 41–47.

7
RESEARCH TOOLS

Introduction

In this chapter, we present a case for the idea of keeping field notes whenever a researcher undertakes a new inquiry and as a tool to support the day-to-day activities of research. We know from experiences of teaching higher education research methods that the idea of the field notebook is not intuitive, even though this tool is commonplace in science and some social science subjects. However, we argue that the notebook can be a central repository of data and a deliberative space for scholarship that changes the quality of thinking and so the research outcomes. Keeping a field notebook also brings a sense of discipline and systematic rigor to the research process. Field notes can form a historical repository of ideas that provide valuable lessons, and can show how thinking has evolved over time. Importantly, the accounts contained in field notes can sometimes be used as a valid source of data in most forms of qualitative research.

This topic is under-theorized in higher education and is seldom addressed in any detail in research methods books. However, field notebooks are commonly used as a method for data collection in action research (McKernan, 1991), anthropology (Sanjek, 1990) and ethnography research (Emerson et al., 2011) and more broadly across the social sciences where observational studies are used. Much can be learned from these accounts but they tend to inform only the systematic use of field notes as primary or secondary sources of data in field studies (Marshall & Rossman, 2014) or as diaries to aid reflection (Drummer et al, 2008). We will address both the use of field notes in field studies and their use in providing a space for reflection and learning.

We have found researchers initially find these ideas difficult until they have experienced using a notebook over time. The purpose of this chapter is to summarize the advantages and the rationale for the field notebook as a research tool to help the new researcher understand what can be gained. One of us uses a hardback notebook while the other uses digital tools for the same purposes. For this chapter, we would like the reader to imagine the notebook we are discussing is more traditional and requires a pen or pencil to make an entry. The chapter is divided into five parts that seek to make the case for the field notebook as an essential part of the research process. These are:

1   Tools for the qualitative researcher
2   A multi-tool
3   Discipline
4   Reflections as a source of data
5   A sense of identity

1 Tools for the qualitative researcher

The study of higher education requires a networked computer, a tape recorder and a field notebook (and little else). In fact, the field notebook can be digital and the recorder a smartphone. So there is not much equipment required. A computer linked to a good library that holds the major journals and books is key to efficiently accessing published peer reviewed journal articles and books. Software to manage qualitative data and analysis or referencing systems are commonplace, and there are good survey tools, databases and easy-to-use statistical packages. These are all so embedded (at least in privileged universities in developed countries) and straightforward that they can nearly be taken for granted, such are the advances in technology. We see some researchers placing a high value on analysis tools, whereas others prefer to do this task themselves. Our experience as supervisors and teachers shows that some tools suit some researchers but for others these can be detrimental to learning. We would never discourage anyone from experimenting with digital tools but care must be taken in case they get in the way of critical and creative thinking.

> Field notes are indispensable in the research process. I keep field notes during data collection and analysis, mostly in digital form. Field notes help me capture context and rationale for decisions I make throughout the research process. If carefully documented, they form an important part of data.
>
> *(New higher education researcher)*

The term 'field' has many different meanings, but in the context of research it is either a branch of study or perhaps a profession, or it refers to work carried out in the natural environment (as opposed to work in a laboratory). In the context of research methods in higher education, we generally refer to the first meaning and refer to the discipline. The researcher is working in a field of interest; however, they can still enter the field quite literally as they visit different sites to collect data. These sites may be, for example, lecture theatres, a lecturer's office or different universities.

> **19 August 2016**
>
> As a science researcher who studied marine ecology, I worked in the laboratory and in the field, mainly doing experimental studies across the oceans of the world. As a student I was trained to keep a meticulous field and laboratory notebook and understood this as part of the validation processes of scientific research. Methods were outlined and contextual data were included, such as date, time and general environmental conditions. Often sketches and maps of study sites would be included; anything that might have some bearing on the research. The dates gave the whole exercise a 'diary' type of feel.
>
> Then the data I collected would be entered and, from time to time, a preliminary statistical analysis done. The notebook would also include general natural history observations that went beyond the study and sometimes I included personal reflections.
>
> My notebooks had hard covers and fitted into a large coat pocket or backpack. The entries were written in pencil (because ink doesn't work well when it's raining or if the pages get damp with sea water). There were advantages and disadvantages to this approach. An advantage would be that the notebook could go places a computer could not, but then the data had to be re-entered into a data base and so transcription errors could happen with this extra step. However, I liked having a hard copy of the research information and had a collection of notebooks on a shelf in my office. In theory, I could have started an analysis again from scratch from the information in the books.
>
> I was always terrified of losing a book and know that data in digital repositories with cloud computing offers much more security. I still use paper, but also take advantage of all possible digital options because data is so hard won and precious, and good ideas need to be captured. Over the years I have been frightened by many stories about losses. The only copy of a typed thesis left on a bus; the computer crash with no back up. We have all heard such stories that serve to warn us about careless research habits.
>
> When I moved from science to join a higher education research group, I was delighted to find that these social scientists also worked with a field notebook. 'Field' was no longer a physical place to go, but a branch of study where I travelled in my mind. Yet I soon came to realise that the principal rationale for science and social science was identical.

FIGURE 7.1 Reflections on the science field notebook

So we have a field of study and may also have field sites to visit. Whenever a project is underway the notebook is a tool used to help with inquiries (see Figure 7.1).

2 A multi-tool

Tools seldom have a single function and a good tool will often serve many needs. Here we look at the field notebook as part of an active research process used during data gathering.

Observational studies

If inquiries are observational, then there are clear procedures that can inform the structural basis of notebook entries (Table 7.1). These types of observational studies

TABLE 7.1 Categories of field note entries for observational studies (after McKernan, 1991)

Field note type	Description	Meaning
Observations	What you saw	Accurate representation of observations
Procedures	What you did	Methods that can be followed by others
Concepts	What you thought	Conceptual thinking that links observations with significant ideas for new theory construction

may also involve video and audio recording of events (such as a lecture or tutorial) but full notes accompany these digital resources.

Using the notebook in interviews

The notebook can also be used before, during and after interviews. The interview is the most common form of collecting qualitative data and taking notes during the interview can help with the process, particularly for semi-structured and open interviews. If a set of questions is to be asked of all participants in a structured interview, then observational notes during the interview will tend to focus on what the researcher sees and any conceptual thoughts that occur at the time. If there is interviewer–respondent interaction with the intention to explore ideas, sometimes it is good to jot down new thoughts and questions as they occur and address these later at a more appropriate point of the interview. A new idea for the interviewer can interrupt the participant's train of thought if asked at the wrong moment. Yet if it is not written down, the interviewer may forget the insight as time passes. We would add that the interviewer should ask the respondent if he or she is comfortable with notes being taken during the interview, as the process itself can be distracting for some.

The field notebook can be used in planning for each interview but it is also equally important to set aside time after the event to focus on writing personal reflections of what has just occurred. Of course, these reflections may be added to at a later date as new thoughts occur.

When reading published research

There are different aims for reading about a subject. A full literature review requires in-depth critique and analysis of articles and books and the notebook is unlikely to play a major part. However, in any analysis of published research, there are significant ideas that emerge that can be crucial to the work in hand or future research. These key thoughts need to be captured and fully referenced (with page numbers where appropriate). Referencing tools can be part of this task but the disadvantage of digital collections is that everything that can be included in a physical notebook will not be kept in one place (typically several digital tools are used) and it requires a good memory and systematic work practices to know where the various notes, data and analyses have been stored and how they can be brought together.

What you hear and who you meet

When a researcher is engaged in conversations with colleagues, involved in group discussions, or listening to a seminar or conference presentation, it sometimes pays to jot down what has been learned in the notebook. After the sessions, reflections can be added and connections made with broader ideas. At a conference it is also handy to write about meeting new colleagues and construct personal profiles. Details can include: institution, research field, latest ideas, shared ideas, information about people in common and personal anecdotes. This advice may seem 'overkill' at the start of a research career but as time progresses, especially for the good networker, it soon becomes apparent that many hundreds of academics will be encountered and it is extremely difficult to remember who they all are. When returning to a conference or re-visiting an institution, read over notes from the previous visit to refresh one's memory. Those who work in the institution are likely to remember you, and they will appreciate you remembering who they are and what they do. Your research community are a vital part of your research projects and so these must be nurtured, even if this requires some support from field notes.

Use in teaching

If research informs teaching, then the notebook can also be used with teaching as an end goal. Considering what might feed into teaching as well as research can help when lectures are brought up to date. In a similar fashion, post-teaching reflections (what went well in class, what can be improved, and so on) can also find a place in the research notebook so that the research lecturer has only one single place for jotting down all their thoughts and ideas.

3 Discipline

Research is a systematic inquiry made public (Stenhouse, 1981 and Chapter 11), and there is a huge difference between systematic and non-systematic inquiries. The first speaks of rigour and careful planning and execution, while work that is non-systematic lends itself to chance and haphazard execution. However, in any inquiry, there will be a degree of randomness in which assumptions have not turned out to be correct, or when new lines of questioning suddenly seem much more appropriate in an interview and the well-thought-out protocol has to be abandoned. What can help is the documenting of the research process in the field notebook, which then allows some structure to be placed on the often messy business of doing research. It is the careful use of the notebook that adds an essential systematic layer to the inquiry. We would also suggest that the discipline required for fine-grained documentation is part of the formation of the critical mind and part of the creative process. The space for creativity is always on offer at the point of making a notebook entry.

Of course, the researcher will not always carry a book around and entries can be made on separate sheets of paper or scribbled on whatever is to hand. These can then be cut and pasted into the notebook later. But the digital world means even this will be a redundant idea for many, as we all seem to carry small computers around that are great for jotting down thoughts and ideas. In fact, a smartphone could probably double as a field notebook in most respects.

4 Reflections as a source of data

Field notebooks have multiple purposes, but the ultimate aim is to improve the quality of the research. In this sense, they are about the researcher's learning and part of the process is critical reflection. The reflective diary has long been a part of action research (Holly, 1989) with the questioning of the 'self' in the sense of self-critical inquiry. This idea has relevance in qualitative research based on hermeneutic principles, because every stage depends on how the individual thinks and acts. Donald Schön (1987) talks about reflection *on* action and reflection *in* action. However, there is also a third dimension: reflection *for* action. So ideas can emerge from what we have been doing and thinking, or what we are planning, and all can be captured in writing in the notebook. In addition, reflections can be entered as we are working (say in an interview). The reflections for action are more about the future and creating a particular deliberative space that focuses the mind for critical thinking.

Deliberative spaces for thinking are becoming harder to find in academic life and the discipline of sitting down to write can be a conduit for making time and space available for transforming our experiences into text. It is a similar sort of space to writing a journal article or book chapter, where the task at hand requires a degree of criticality, creativity and dedication. Moon (2006) suggests that writing 'slows down' the pace of learning and although 'deliberative' sounds like the event must be lengthy, it will mostly consist of short periods of time when good ideas occur or when that very rare eureka moment happens. These spaces can seem more mundane around planning, for example, with lists of tasks to do. However, it does take time to re-read field note reflections, although now and again this will pay dividends for learning.

Field note reflections are a valid source of data that can be incorporated directly into a publication or supplement other forms of data. Notes can be used to triangulate or confirm other data sources. In addition, sometimes a researcher has to return to the field itself when data are missing (Corbin and Strauss, 1990). For example, the researcher can be reading an interview transcript and realize that a response is important for the study but the meaning is not clear. If the field notes do not help in understanding and interpretation, then the researcher can go back to the respondent and ask the question again or seek clarification (Chapter 9).

Conclusion

Using a field notebook contributes in a small way to creating a sense of researcher identity. Typically, identity in the context of research is about the researcher's voice in the research process and final written account. However, in this case we are arguing for the field notebook as a tool or artefact that forms part of the researcher's technological apparatus that has an impact on professional identity. These tools add value to 'being a researcher' because they add rigour to the research process and provide opportunities for altering the quality of thought. Yet tools can also counter the hegemonic positivist views that qualitative research in an educational field has less worth than quantitative research. Although the experienced researcher will ignore such a false dichotomy, the reactions of those new to higher education are quite different and any tool that helps the new researcher experience and understand the systematic nature of an inquiry can help change what we regard as an unhealthy perception. In this sense, the field notebook is part of becoming a higher education researcher.

Yet there is also something symbolic about the field notebook in its equivalence to the scientific field or laboratory notebook. In the same way, it is becoming more common to call a higher education research group a 'research laboratory'. Borrowing terms from science is both political and about changing the perceptions of those who may not value what we do.

Bibliography

Corbin, J.M. & Strauss, A. (1990). Grounded theory research: Procedures, canons, and evaluative criteria, *Qualitative Sociology*, 13, 1: 3–21.

Drummer, T.J.B., Cook, I.G., Parker, S.L., Barrett, G.A. & Hull, A.P. (2008). Promoting and assessing 'deep learning' in geography fieldwork: An evaluation of reflective diaries, *Journal of Geography in Higher Education*, 32, 3: 459–479.

Emerson, R.M., Fretz, R.I. &. Shaw, L.L. (2011). *Writing ethnographic fieldnotes*. Chicago, IL: University of Chicago Press.

Holly, M.L. (1989). Reflective writing and the spirit of inquiry, *Cambridge Journal of Education*, 19, 1: 71–80.

Marshall, C. & Rossman. G.B. (2014). *Designing qualitative research*. Thousand Oaks, CA: Sage.

McKernan, J. (1991). *Curriculum action research: A handbook of methods and resources for the reflective practitioner*. London, UK: Kogan Page.

Moon, J.A. (2006). *Learning journals: A handbook for reflective practice and professional development*. London, UK: Routledge.

Sanjek, R. (1990). *Fieldnotes: The makings of anthropology*. Ithaca, NY: Cornell University Press.

Schön, D. (1987). *Educating the reflective practitioner*. San Francisco, CA: Jossey-Bass Publishers.

Stenhouse, L. (1981). What counts as research? *British Journal of Educational Studies*, 14, 2: 103–114.

8
ENGAGING WITH THE LITERATURE

Introduction

Getting to know a subject and creating new concepts and theories requires a deep understanding of what has already been published. To obtain this knowledge entails engaging with what is loosely termed 'the literature'. Often this task is described as doing a 'literature review', but this is only one form of engagement. Of course academics are naturally interested in their subject and reading published work is necessary to further develop subject knowledge and expertise. However, a literature review is also done for a wide variety of reasons that can be quite specific. In this chapter, we have considered the following purposes:

1 To understand the field and help develop a research question or identify a worthwhile gap.
2 To provide the context and justification for a study in the introductory section of a journal article or thesis and allow for comparative and critical analysis of data.
3 To demonstrate knowledge and insight into a subject for the purposes of a gaining a PhD and writing a thesis.
4 To conduct a systematic review of a research topic.

These four purposes share many of the same features and require similar skills. Regardless of what type of review is involved, we know that novice researchers find all forms of engaging with the literature a challenge. In our view, those new to research can easily replicate what is said in published accounts but find it difficult to extract useful concepts. A further challenge comes from the field itself. The subject of higher education is vast and multi-disciplinary and those new to the subject, and in particular those who are also new to research, have a tendency to read published work (regardless of purpose) without knowing when to stop. We think that this continual reading phenomenon is attributed to several drivers. First, the novice may find it difficult to extract the more useful conceptual ideas from each article and so will go on to the next in the hope that something important will eventually emerge through this process. In this sense, reviewing the literature is a numbers game that may also be driven by the fear of missing out on something important. Second, there are lots of interesting ideas to be discovered and these can all seem relevant to a new researcher. The researcher's enthusiasm for collecting such ideas causes the subject to expand exponentially and with it the reading task. Knowing when something is peripheral or tangential to a study is a skill usually learned through time and experience, but we suggest that lack of analytical skills, being enthusiastic and making poor judgements may all be reinforced by procrastination. It is easier to defer the more critical and conceptual aspects of research and keep busy by continuing to read on.

To engage with the literature in a timely manner and approach it critically is essential to any research apprenticeship. In this chapter, we propose that the required analytical skills can be learned in a systematic way, and that once learned, will influence all aspects of research and being a researcher. Ideally, the review of the literature comes to an end when the researcher no longer sees any new ideas that can contribute to a study. This state could be referred to as a 'point of saturation', which is similar to the same concept used in determining the number of qualitative interviews required in a study (Chapter 5). However, time or resources usually determine the point of saturation and we call this 'executive saturation', meaning that the researcher makes an executive decision to stop reading the literature, while fully aware that this would continue under more ideal conditions.

Academics who are already experienced in a research field should have no problem engaging with literature in higher education. However, we suggest that this chapter may still be of some use here, because the structured system we outline and the tools provided may be used for supervision and training postgraduate student researchers in various fields. Most postgraduates have little research experience and are likely to be weak in this area. Essentially, we are recommending that novices should be trained systematically in the procedures for review, and once these initial skills have been mastered, they can be put to use in the various forms of literature engagement that occur throughout a research project. As expertise is developed, a lot of what we outline here will become more instinctive and perhaps even taken for granted.

The chapter is organized into three sections. In Section 1, we look at the key knowledge outcome of a literature review and provide a model for developing a conceptual framework. Section 2 presents a model for a systematic process for literature review. In Section 3, we provide two simple tools to help novice researchers organize their ideas, and some thoughts about how an expert might approach the literature.

1 Developing a conceptual framework

Not only do researchers need to know and understand their field, identify a meaningful gap and develop a research question, it is important that a conceptual framework is developed. This framework contributes to theory development and is usually determined and refined through engagement with the literature. For example, the concept 'powerful knowledge' is currently a topic of renewed interest in higher education research and there are several authors writing about it, but framing it in different conceptual ways (Wheelahan, 2015; Young, 2013; Young & Muller 2013). We use this example because it has recently challenged us and we know what steps we had to take in order to tease out the various meanings in order to (hopefully) make a contribution to the theory. First we needed to examine the relevant literature and carefully identify the components of this concept, work out how different authors defined these, how they differed and how they related to each other. Each element had to be understood and clearly described (in writing) to arrive at a precise meaning. Once we had a definition (which was not always possible), the elements had to be compared and their relationship to the wider theoretical claims clarified. We then developed a set of diagrams that led to a model that represented our developing thoughts around the concept. These abstract ideas about the process are illustrated and mapped out step-wise in Figure 8.1.

We suggest that the steps will be second nature to an experienced researcher, but a useful guide to the novice, and a reminder that concept formation should always be at the forefront of a research project, with established theory having a central role in this process. The method outlined in Figure 8.1 contains procedural elements, however abstract they may seem, and using these systematically can provide scaffolding for this key skill. Providing *systematic* ways of learning how to review the literature is the main theme for this chapter.

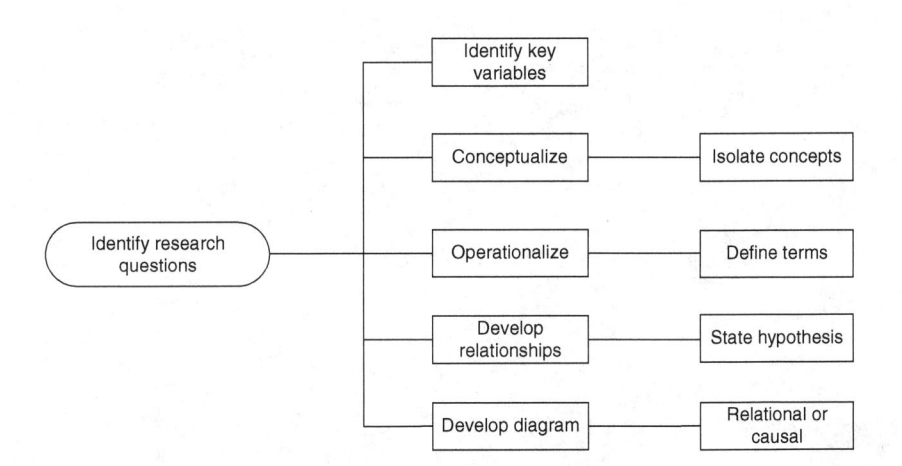

FIGURE 8.1 Steps in developing a conceptual framework

2 How to engage systematically with the literature

In this section, we present a model for engaging with the literature. There are two steps. The first looks at how a researcher selects which articles to read, compiles summary abstracts and validates these. This stage is very similar to the procedure used in systematic literature reviews (see the further reading section at the end of the book). The second step is about the review itself and this is done in three dimensions that consist of description, synthesis and critique. We call the second stage the 'tripartite approach' and present a model that combines the two stages as a structured systematic guide. Once mastered, the skills can be used every time a researcher reads a journal article or book, regardless of the purpose of doing so.

Framing a research area for review

In this process, a researcher begins by identifying an area of investigation and establishes the context and purpose for the review. Quite often, purpose and context can be directly drawn from a research statement or question; however, in qualitative research this question may alter as the review progresses. The first step in framing is to follow the procedures for a systematic review of a research topic and develop inclusion and exclusion criteria for selecting materials. This process should yield all the published material on a topic (with respect to the criteria of interest) (see Figure 8.2).

Once the purpose of the study is clear and criteria for locating and including materials for the review finalized, screening the literature begins. Screening materials entails identifying and categorizing published work and establishing what constitutes 'relevant' materials for the review. A search strategy requires the formulation

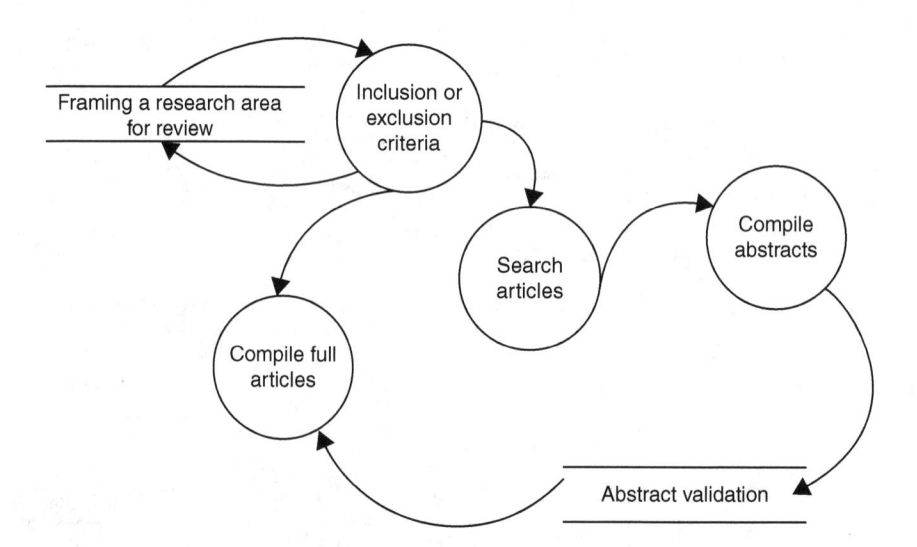

FIGURE 8.2 Framing a research area for review

of concrete search terms and for new researchers (especially postgraduate students), we highly recommend seeking the guidance of a subject librarian with expertise in this area. Most academic materials are indexed and archived in different online databases, with the most notable of these being: Google Scholar, ISI proceedings, PsycINFO, EBSCOHost, JSTOR, Cochrane Reviews, Medline, Scopus, and Web of Science. Further investigation needs be done from the initial search, because a database will provide a link for each article that has cited the research since the original article's publication. Of course the reference list at the end of each article lets the reader know who the author has cited. Writing summaries or 'abstracts' of each paper is essential (see Section 3 of this chapter on 'tools'). These abstracts can then be checked against the inclusion and exclusion criteria and validated through relevance to the overall purpose of the review.

Review process

There are three stages in the review process (Figure 8.3).

Tripartite I (description)

In this stage, the systematic reviews are examined firstly to present a descriptive summary of the key issues identified. This process should give an overview of developments in the field, the main areas of debate and the outstanding research questions. The overview is usually followed by the presentation of identified themes that have been carefully justified.

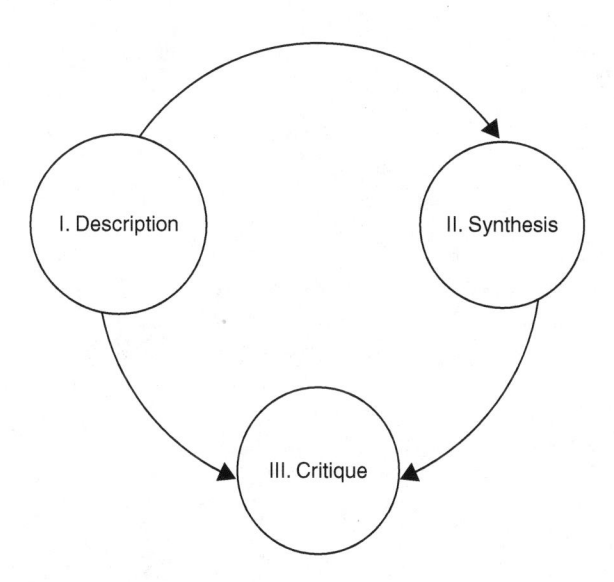

FIGURE 8.3 The review process

Tripartite II (synthesis)

In the second part of the review process, the researcher focuses on the synthesis of ideas. To do this requires the extraction of selected ideas or themes and a process of comparing and contrasting these to identify areas of similarity, difference and any controversies. Synthesis allows the researcher to clarify and resolve inconsistencies in thinking or tensions in the literature and thereby provides the best chance of making a genuine contribution to knowledge in the field. Through synthesis, the researcher places the topic or problem in perspective within the literature, demonstrates that he or she understands the broader field in which the research is situated, and that the particular problem of interest can be contextualized within the historical context of which the subject is being studied.

Tripartite III (critique)

In the third phase, the researcher reflects on the synthesis of the main ideas identified at the second stage, then develops a critical view of work reviewed in the light of claims and evidence available. It is important that there is validation of selected material and that it has been described correctly. It is only after thorough description and summary that a level of critical thinking and judgement can later be applied. Critical engagement requires the development of particular skills and strategies, and it particularly implies having the ability to closely examine claims against alternative evidence or views. It also requires a questioning mind and an openness to alternative views or evidence from other sources. Critique should include a positive dimension as the researcher aims to provide new ideas and alternatives. This attitude of mind contrasts with the idea of being critical in the sense of being dismissive. We make this point because we have observed novices being dismissively critical without being constructive. In the final literature report, there should be an account that includes the implications of the analysis.

The tripartite model

When the two parts (Figures 8.2 and 8.3) of the model are brought together, there is a full systematic process that a new researcher can follow to conduct a literature review (Figure 8.4). The components of the model and step-by-step process provide a checklist; however, the model also provides a schematic representation of the relationship between the different model elements.

3 Tools for reviewing the literature

It has been suggested by Onwuegbuzie and Weinbaum (2017) that there are two main ways to systematically examine the literature: the within-study analysis and the between-study analysis. These can provide an alternative to, or form part of, the tripartite model. Both within and between methods of analyses are done for

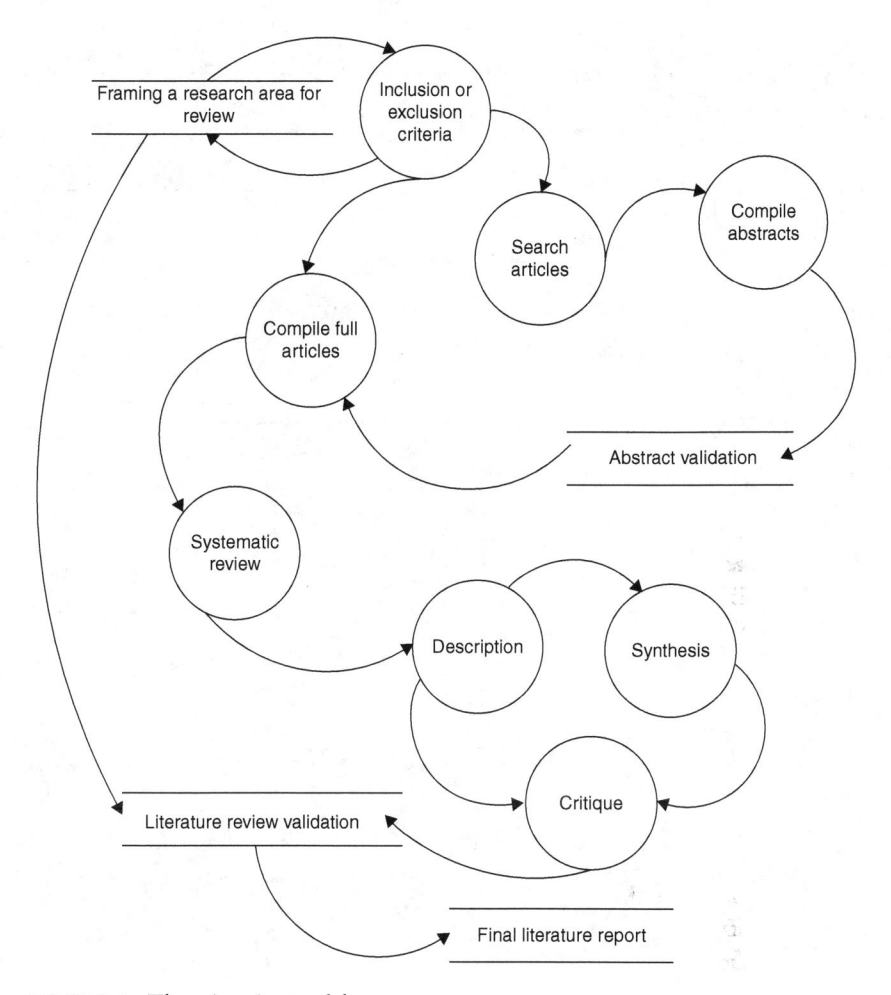

FIGURE 8.4 The tripartite model

the purpose of producing a more critical and engaging report of the literature. Of course, if this outcome does not eventuate, then the tools proposed will not have fulfilled their purpose and so have little utility. We provide an example of how a within-study analysis can be done, and then an example of a between-study analysis that is focused on synthesis of ideas in the literature.

Within-study analysis

The within-study analysis involves analysis of the entire content of a single article including the title, literature review section, conceptual/theoretical framework, procedures used, results and discussion (Onwuegbuzie & Weinbaum, 2010; see Table 8.1). It is systematic and comprehensive, going beyond the review abstract in the tripartite model, and includes a summary of findings and conclusions reached.

TABLE 8.1 Within-study analysis

Elements reviewed	Articles reviewed				
	Article $_1$	Article $_2$	Article $_3$	Article $_4$	Article ...$_n$
Aims/objectives					
Research questions					
Methods					
Theory					
Conclusions					
Limitations					
So what?					

This type of analysis is similar to doing a peer review of a journal article or a book review. A within-study analysis begins with identifying the aims of each article, the questions raised, methods used in answering the questions, and the theory that the authors draw from, as well as the conclusions reached.

An example of how this structure might be used is given in the box below in a within-study analysis of a journal article from 2007.

EXAMPLE OF A WITHIN-STUDY ANALYSIS

Article reviewed

Rayle, A.D. & Chung, K.Y. (2007). Revisiting first-year college students' mattering: Social support, academic stress, and the mattering experience, *Journal of College Student Retention: Research, Theory & Practice*, 9, 1: 21–37.

Aims/objectives

The purpose of this study was to investigate the concept of student 'mattering' and defining it. Concepts comprise students feeling included by their peers, feeling they were important to the institution and feeling supported by family. This is not a novel concept and the authors admit this in the first sentence of the abstract where they state they are revisiting a previously discussed theory from Nancy Schlossberg.

Research questions

Does social support from friends and family predict mattering to university friends and the institution? Does social support from friends and family, and mattering to university friends and to the institution relate to a level of academic stress? Do male and female students differ in social support, academic stress, and mattering to university friends and the institution?

Methods

This research utilized three survey instruments, two of which were established, and the third created by one of the authors. First, the perceived social support inventory-friend scale (PSS-Fr) and family scale (PSS-Fa) assessed the perception of support from both family and friends. The Daily Hassles Index for College Stress (DHI) was then used to assess academic stress, and finally, the Interpersonal and General Mattering Assessment (IGMA) was used to assess the sense of mattering to others. Participants were recruited using a convenience sampling method, where all students were invited to participate. They were given time to complete the surveys during class resulting in a response rate of ~87%.

Theory

The study draws on a link between social support from both family and university friends to the perceived amount of mattering. Regarding feeling included in the university environment, the most important link discovered was between the social support of friends and the university environment. These two phenomena (family and university friends) could predict academic stress levels. The more social support, and the more support from family and friends, the less likely students were to be stressed in their first year. Gender was also a strong contributor to academic stress and feelings of mattering. Females felt like they mattered more to family and friends, and reported higher levels of academic stress.

Conclusions

Social support from family and friends is essential in developing a sense of belonging or mattering in a university environment, but equally importantly the development of new social networks and new friends contributes to decreased levels of academic stress once at university. Females tend to feel the stresses of academic life more acutely, as they feel like they matter more to their family and social support networks. In this sense, mattering has both positive and negative connotations.

Limitations

This study was limited to students from one first-year course at one university in the US. It only utilized established surveys, rather than surveys and interviews. These surveys will provide a limited range of views and responses.

So what?

This work builds on earlier studies by investigating this concept of 'mattering', where it is evident that forming new relationships and social support is just as critical as having existing family and friend support. Probably the most important contribution is in the different pressures that male and female students experience as part of their first year at university and suggestions on ways to minimize this.

TABLE 8.2 Synthesis of the articles reviewed

Elements reviewed	Articles reviewed		
	Group...$_1$(articles)	Group...$_2$(articles)	Group... $_n$(articles)
Summary Shared conclusions Contrasting views Current debates Outstanding questions			

Between-study analysis

In contrast to the within-study procedure, a between-study literature analysis involves comparing and contrasting key findings or summaries from more than one source of literature. When there are multiple concepts or questions to be considered in a research project, then a systematic grouping of articles can be performed. Usually the researcher is interested in the common concepts related to the research question and so will focus on specific article elements. In this way, an analysis can be done either 'by group' or 'by element'. So in Table 8.2, the focus could be on comparing all the group 1 articles with group 3, or on a synthesis of the summaries or conclusions from all groups.

4 A non-systematic approach

This example is not a tool or an approach but is included to contrast the structured methods of review with what might happen when the researcher has been reading in the literature for a number of years. Our inquiries have shown that those with more experience in research often find it difficult to explain how they approach the literature, and therefore in Figure 8.5 we provide a short written reflection that captures the lived experience of engaging with the literature and carrying out research. When we are teaching this part of research methodology, we often find the sorts of decisions we have made in our own work hard to describe. It is partly for this reason that we developed the tripartite model.

Conclusion

Engaging with the literature prior to data collection or theory development is a significant undertaking. A review allows depth and breadth of knowledge to be developed in a particular subject and highlights knowledge trends and existing academic debates and helps frame important research questions. Importantly, the process of review is crucial to concept formation, which is essential to guide the full research process and contribute to new theory. A review of the literature involves

Background

As a research scientist, I knew every paper written in my highly specialized subject from the late 1800s to the latest articles. I read them all from cover to cover. They were printed, kept in boxes labelled A to Z and so formed my reference collection. When I later started higher education research, this simple working convention did not apply to my new field. In particular, I could not find established independent groups of researchers, working in the same subject and who built on each other's findings and theories. Whenever I thought I had found such a group, I realized that each researcher or team was essentially working independently, typically in unique contexts, and at best drawing on parts of others' work to support their own findings. So whichever higher education subject I was interested in, nearly all the journal articles on that subject could add something to what I already knew, but seldom had the power to transform my thinking (in the sense that I would understand the field in a radically different way). In other words, few articles have ever had anything worthwhile to say to me, although most would contribute in a small way to my research. The few that have something worthwhile to say are precious. Of course this is not a problem for the research itself, nor is it caused by my high expectations of others' work. I think it is because I approach the work I do with a conceptual idea already framed. Let me give two examples that might illustrate this.

Conceptual ideas

I generally start with a conceptual idea because it seems to me the best way of making a theoretical contribution to knowledge. In this context, I seek research that will help me to achieve this goal. My strategy includes quickly skim reading small parts of many journal articles that appear to be written on the same topic. If the article seems promising, then I might carefully read the last paragraph of the conclusion. If there is something in this, with respect to my conceptual thinking, then the article gets more attention. I do the same for books and chapters but the skim reading takes a little longer (although I get a lot of help from keyword searches in a PDF viewer). I then explore other knowledge fields that I have a hunch might also contribute to my central idea. These typically include reading in areas such as philosophy, history, sociology and, less frequently, psychology. I also have a high respect for quality journalism and have also learned much from novelists who often have very interesting things to say about the human condition. And then I learn from the many conversations I have with colleagues about what I am trying to work out, and the feedback I get from seminars and conference presentations.

Applying established theories

A second approach is when I am seeking to understand an established theory and apply this in research and practice. Then I read everything on this theory: all the articles and books from start to finish, frequently re-reading them many times. It feels much more like being a scientist in this sense, although I do find that the casual use of the English language often leaves me guessing if different authors are really talking about the same thing. Interpretation of meaning then becomes part of this challenge but the rewards for effort seem to be high.

The hunt

So I see myself as a hunter tracking down ideas that will help me achieve my goal, and like any hunter, I have more than one strategy for conducting the chase. And although I may not always be successful, the effort is never wasted because something is learned and more experience gained. In this sense, what comes from my experiences of reading the literature will help me now or later, and no doubt form part of my subconscious that allows my thinking to progress. Holding on to this belief means I never feel that I am wasting my time.

FIGURE 8.5 Hunting for knowledge

gaining not only new knowledge but also analytical skills that can be put to use in a broad range of contexts. Facility for grasping the nature and use of argument and critical thinking all come from purposefully reading to gain a deeper understanding of ideas.

We have structured this chapter around the central idea that systematically engaging with the literature using structured approaches is the best way for those new to research and the study of higher education to learn. Our experiences of teaching research methods have clearly illustrated the difficulties this group faces when it comes to reading and engaging with published work. We have used the tripartite model to good effect and because students and academic staff have found it useful, we have some confidence in its broader utility. In particular, we think that it will have utility for learning about all forms of literature engagement, although this claim has not been tested.

In a practical sense, undertaking a literature review is necessary because without it one cannot evidence or justify the need to undertake any research, and it would be impossible to argue for a 'gap' in the literature. We address gap statements in Chapter 12, but include here a list of fallacies that we see in articles as justification for the importance of research. However, these must also be understood in the context of how articles are cited and so they are important ideas when reviewing and criticizing the literature. The fallacies are:

- Appeal to exaggerated research gap (nothing is known)
- Appeal to volume (multiple citing of unnecessary, unrelated or inconsequential work)
- Appeal to history (using historical knowledge to justify the rationale for carrying out a study)
- Appeal to emotions (soliciting credibility based on emotions)
- Appeal to authority (using the well-known figure to substantiate arguments rather than the worth of an argument)
- Appeal to fame (just because a piece of evidence is famous does not make it credible)
- Appeal to admiration (citing work based on friendship, acquaintance and respect)

If none of the systematic approaches to literature appeals, then one idea to consider is to follow Ernest Hemingway's advice and always have your 'crap detector' switched on (Postman & Weingartner, 1969). This colourful metaphor creates a critical image for novices and experts alike who should be sceptical about claims, never take them at face value, and always look for ideas based on good evidence or robust argument. For example, and with respect to the literature review, the poor way in which published work can be used and cited in articles is given in Chapter 6 on the single case. Part of a PhD student's training requires that he or she can demonstrate the command of an existing body of knowledge in their field. Students need to show that they are aware of the important debates and relevant research problems, but also recognize that doing a literature review in a critical manner is essential to developing intellectual capability.

Finally, the literature review is a living document and should not be seen as the first part of a study and then compartmentalized as such. Our work in peer review picks out this inconsistency time and again in articles submitted to the journals we review for. Often it seems that the literature review was done first, before the analysis and conclusion were reached, and as such no longer fully aligns with the study. Similarly, a PhD literature review may include a lot of papers and ideas that no longer have any relevance to the project and how it has gradually developed and changed over the intervening years. A literature review should be done first and last and at every stage in between. In other words, re-visit the literature review before the project is deemed complete and ensure that all of it is relevant to the rest of the study being reported. A paper, chapter or thesis should always have some form of logical narrative without taking the reader in an irrelevant direction or providing them with tangential ideas.

Bibliography

Onwuegbuzie, A.J. & Weinbaum, R.K. (2017). A framework for using qualitative comparative analysis for the review of the literature, *The Qualitative Report*, 22, 2: 359–372.

Postman, N. & Weingartner, C. (1969). *Teaching as a subversive activity*. New York, NY: Dell Publishing Company.

Rayle, A.D. & Chung, K.Y. (2007). Revisiting first-year college students' mattering: Social support, academic stress, and the mattering experience, *Journal of College Student Retention: Research, Theory & Practice*, 9, 1: 21–37.

Wheelahan, L. (2015). Not just skills: What a focus on knowledge means for vocational education, *Journal of Curriculum Studies*, 47, 6: 750–762.

Young, M. (2013). Overcoming the crisis in curriculum theory: A knowledge-based approach, *Journal of Curriculum Studies*, 45, 2: 101–118.

Young, M. & Muller, J. (2013). On the powers of powerful knowledge, *Review of Education*, 1, 3: 229–250.

9
QUALITATIVE DATA ANALYSIS

Introduction

Those new to qualitative research face significant challenges when analyzing qualitative data. The problems are particularly acute when it comes to dealing with large numbers of interview transcripts. This chapter provides a visual summary of the qualitative research process and a framework that simplifies the process of analysis. We show how to develop a coding scheme, and discuss different types of coding. Because there are many approaches to coding data, we include a critique of the common ones.

Qualitative research is exploratory in nature and concerned with the examination of narratives and people's interactions within a particular social context. It aims to understand how people construct or make sense of their experiences and the environment in which such experiences are formed, and so differs methodologically from quantitative approaches (Chapter 4; El Hussein, Jakubec & Osuji, 2015; Hartman, 2015). Qualitative researchers frame research questions with respect to the how, why and what. They explore relationships and connections not readily evident in quantitative traditions. Further, within the qualitative tradition, the research process involves identifying a research problem or research goal, often from the viewpoint of the person under study (Schmid, 1981). However, qualitative research still draws on a set of methods and techniques to help achieve critical examination of the phenomena of interest. All parts of the qualitative research process are guided by specific interpretative ontologies (see Chapter 2), and this is particularly relevant to analysis.

Lately, with the permeation of technology into social and natural systems, new forms of data generated by computers, sensors and humans have become available. The growing complexity of this data requires new visual techniques for analysis and representation. Further, because most of the processes and decisions needed to study a particular social phenomenon are complex and multifaceted, visualization

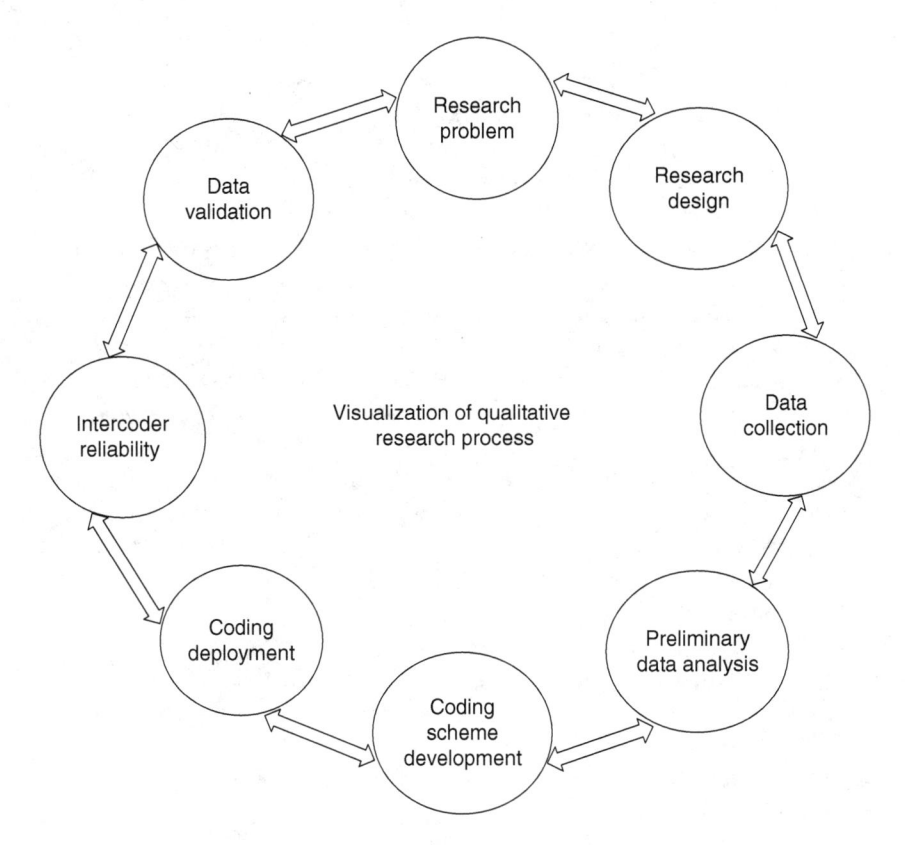

FIGURE 9.1 The process of undertaking qualitative research

can capture this complexity and present ideas in a more intuitive way for researchers. As an example, Figure 9.1 shows a visual presentation of the processes involved in undertaking a research analysis.

1 Data analysis process

Qualitative data primarily comprises transcripts of text, videos, audios, pictures, automated user online trails, web pages and other documents (Kamalodeen & Jameson-Charles, 2016), as well as hyperlinks and data collected from social media (Snelson, 2016). Qualitative data analysis is broadly conceptualized as a meaning-making process, involving the subjective interpretation of the content of data through the systematic classification process of coding and identifying themes or patterns (Hsieh & Shannon, 2005). It is therefore an empirical, methodical and systematic analysis within a particular context. Qualitative data analysis can also be broadly understood as a reduction and sense-making endeavour that takes a volume of qualitative material and attempts to identify core patterns and meanings (Patton, 2002).

The majority of the techniques for analysis have no clear conventions or procedures but we conceptualize the process as having two stages. The first is very rapid and leads to the main themes and a tentative conclusion. The second comes through writing about the themes in a recursive process that requires revisiting the data and theory, using a critical lens and creative thinking as new ideas and concepts are formed. If this two-stage approach is accepted procedurally, then it helps researchers to move ahead in a timely fashion and avoid what can be experienced as a daunting and stressful analytical process lasting many months. We advise our postgraduates that after an initial reading of interview transcripts (for example), the main themes are mapped out. Each of these themes should be named, have a description of what they are about and include relevant quotes from the data. Once this preliminary framework has been developed, then the student can move on to the second stage of analysis.

The process of analyzing qualitative data is iterative and systematic in nature (Ritchie & Spencer, 2002; Thomas, 2006). It requires a researcher to go through a messy and often variant volume of data and develop codes, themes and theory (O'Dwyer, 2004; Smith & Firth, 2011). Regardless of which analysis strategy is taken, it will require:

- a clear understanding of the phenomenon under study;
- synthesizing data to expose different aspects of the phenomenon under investigation;
- distilling links and relationships between concepts and theory;
- theorizing about how such relationships appear; and
- contextualizing findings within a broader literature.

After the preliminary analysis, the second stage of a typical study can be done in a series of steps summarized in Figure 9.2.

The first two steps of this process are fairly straightforward and involve organizing the data and making sure it is all clearly understood. If further clarification is required, it is often possible to contact a respondent again and start a new dialogue. This procedure can be done by email or other means and can be an important step that is typically thought of as 'not permitted' by the novice. Qualitative research, unlike most quantitative studies, is never a one-shot endeavour and many of the 'rules' are more like guidelines that can change depending on circumstances. The important point here is that all steps and procedures are clearly stated in the method section of a report.

2 Coding qualitative data

Researchers employing interpretative research paradigms often collect a variety of qualitative data using instruments such as interviews (structured, semi-structured and open) and focus groups, carried out in a variety of settings. In addition, there are observational notes, secondary data, transcripts of discourses, film, social media,

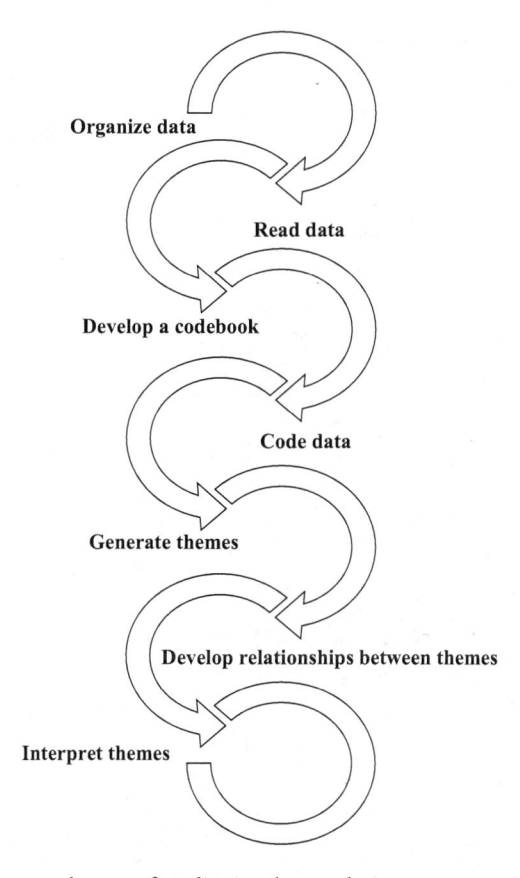

- Organize data
- Read data
- Develop a codebook
- Code data
- Generate themes
- Develop relationships between themes
- Interpret themes

FIGURE 9.2 The second stage of qualitative data analysis

photographs, maps and more. Making sense of these data requires coding. In stage two of an analysis, the themes already discerned need to be refined. If this is done systematically (with a gesture towards being objective), then a researcher needs to bracket out any pre-conceived ideas before he or she starts. Identification of the main themes is then done through a systematic assignment of codes. Coding entails attaching labels or codes to text that eventually represent the study themes (Basit, 2003). It requires organizing data into units, and the development of a coding scheme to guide the process. These steps are shown for interview transcripts in Figure 9.3.

A coding scheme can be based on meaning (semantics) extracted from different levels of units of analysis (sentence, paragraph and message) and the contexts of the interactions. In a semantic analysis, codes are generated from the meaning of the text. Similar texts are grouped into codes and similar codes into clusters. Identifying codes can be iterative and recursive, in that after a block of coding is completed, the emerging codes are then used to review earlier transcripts. In other words, the act of reading, coding, reading and coding happens over time, often between researchers in a team, and in a forward-thinking as well as a retrospective manner.

102 Qualitative data analysis

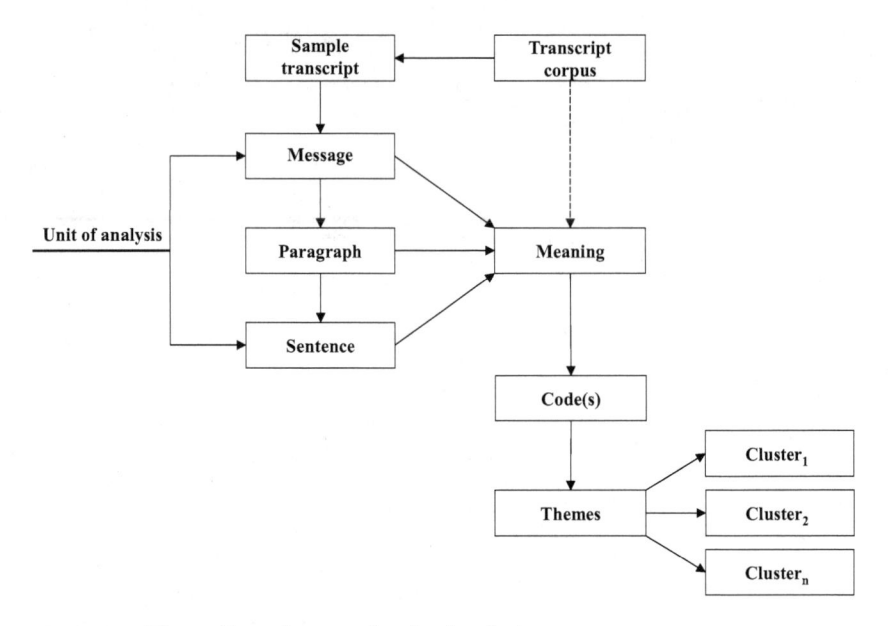

FIGURE 9.3 The coding scheme and unit of analysis

In this model, the researcher can go straight from the transcript corpus to the semantic analysis, which is equivalent to analysis stage one if the process momentarily stops here. Semantic analysis always concerns how the researcher understands the knowledge and ideas. However, a systematic coding process starts by working out the units of analysis though inductive and deductive reasoning and then taking these units from each transcript to form codes and then themes.

Three types of coding can be distinguished: open coding, axial coding and selective coding (Figure 9.4). Open coding is often applied at the beginning of an analysis. It enables researchers to identify codes without necessarily paying attention to sequencing, order, structure and patterns. In the second pass of the process, axial coding requires the relationships among codes to be identified. Selective coding occurs when researchers are interested in examining a particular portion of data to explore features of the phenomenon under study.

The tripled-coding style illustrated in Figure 9.4 is congruent with grounded theory (a common inductive methodology that claims to produce theory that is grounded in the data: see the further reading section at the end of the book). In grounded theory, the application of open coding requires the researcher to describe the data conceptually. For instance, codes are contextualized within the data and based on published theory from the literature. In axial coding, the researcher develops meaning and relationships between concepts. For instance, when coding a concept such as 'attitude', other concepts such as behaviours, beliefs and feelings may be considered as related in some way. At this point, it may also be desirable to engage in coding based on a predetermined theoretical or conceptual framework, to tease out potential explanations for the phenomenon being researched. Selective coding,

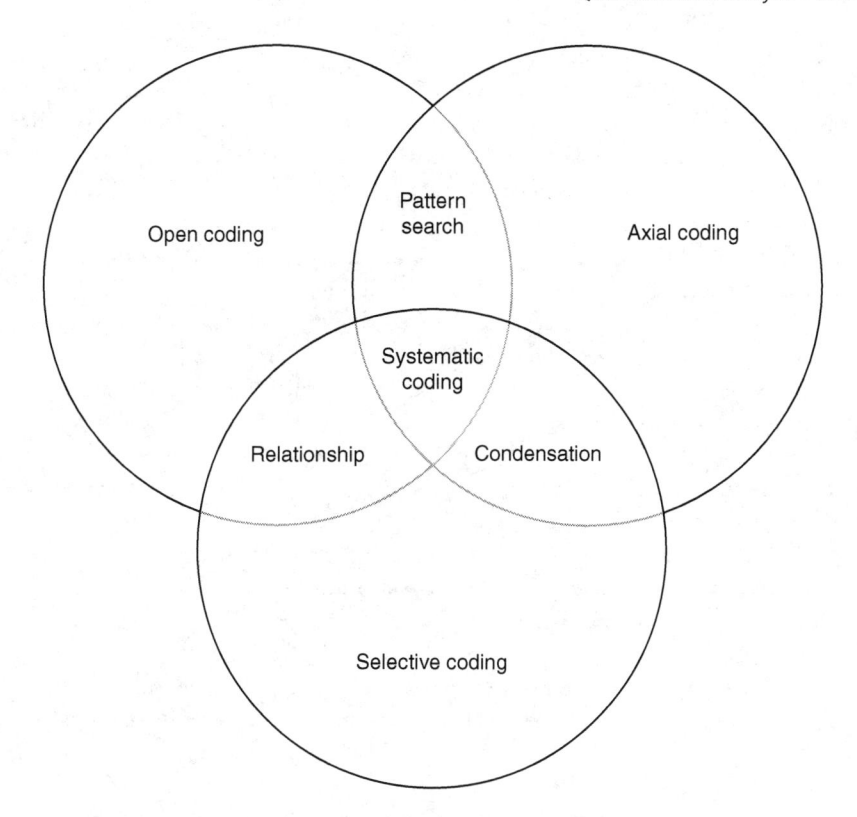

FIGURE 9.4 Triple-coding qualitative analysis

on the other hand, looks for particular categories of codes, relationships and consequences that may or may not be of interest to the researcher or phenomenon under investigation.

Researchers interested in applying triple coding should also learn about the constant comparison technique which is undertaken to observe and compare phenomena in the context of the data, often to create codes that are precise and consistent. Constant comparison presumes that the researcher will engage in a systematic comparison of each code or dataset assigned to a category. Categories are then integrated based on similar properties, again through inductive and deductive reasoning and interpretation. Constant comparison is used in many established qualitative data analysis procedures.

3 Intercoder reliability

In qualitative studies where there are two or more researchers involved in coding the data, intercoder reliability becomes a significant challenge. Intercoder reliability is a quality assurance measure (see Chapter 10) that is concerned with the extent to which independent coders assess the meaning and structure of the same body of text or artefact, and how consistency in meaning is maintained (Auld et al., 2007; Cicchetti, 1976; Gwet, 2014). Intercoder reliability can also be used as an alternative for determining construct validity (Ryan & Ward, 1999), which determines if the claims made are based on the data collected.

The process starts with the first researcher initiating the coding, and the second reviewing what is coded. Intercoder reliability estimates are then calculated using probabilities (e.g. Cohen's kappa coefficient, a statistic used to measure inter-rater agreement on outcomes of assessing a particular phenomenon between at least two researchers). The value obtained is used as a proxy for claims about the accuracy and consistency of the coders or the coded themes in a text. In a situation where there is noticeable disagreement in the coding structure and meaning, negotiation has to be carried out to reach a consensus, or a degree of consensus, depending on the levels of acceptable difference. Once a coding scheme is established, the next step is to select a transcript or body of text to code independently by each researcher. The intercoder reliability value is then calculated. In the event of intercoder reliability being low or when there are discrepancies, negotiation of meaning and interpretation is done so that a shared understanding is reached to provide some form of standardization of definitions and themes.

The frequency of occurrence of themes per transcript between coders can be computed using the following formula: **per cent agreement = agreement/ agreement + disagreement**. Table 9.1 shows how values obtained can be interpreted.

In most cases, low agreement levels suggest that researchers have defined codes too broadly and that these require clarification. However, when complex responses are made to difficult research questions, getting two researchers to agree on interpretation will be difficult and negotiation will inevitably involve compromise. Qualitative research is founded on the principle of interpretation and it is unlikely that two researchers will interpret the world in exactly the same way. In addition, the integrity of research findings is judged by the level of rigour applied to the entire research process. Quality is judged by the contribution the research makes to knowledge and practice.

TABLE 9.1 Threshold per cent agreement levels

Values	Interpretation
0.90	Very good – always acceptable
0.80	Good – acceptable in most situations
0.70	Adequate – acceptable in exploratory studies
0.60	Poor – barely acceptable

Source: Auld et al. (2007).

4 Theoretical approaches to data analysis

Reasoning

Although the process of analyzing qualitative data is complex, we suggest there are three broad methods of reasoning, each with different properties. These are the deductive method, the inductive method, or a combination of both. The deductive approach is often used when a researcher imposes a theoretical structure on to the data and uses this to develop codes, identify patterns and themes. This method is useful in studies where researchers are already aware of possible outcomes of the research, or have well-structured data and obvious participant responses. Deductive reasoning is typically found in pure science and quantitative approaches and is based on the idea that the structure of analysis, coding and procedures are determined by the question and data. Codes are not predetermined by a theoretical framework.

In contrast, an inductive approach is based on inductive reasoning and is more common in studies that have a limited theoretical basis and where broad generalizations are sought from particular observations. In practice, most forms of qualitative higher education analysis require a mix of inductive and deductive reasoning because the research often starts with a theoretical position, but this can change as new ideas emerge from an exploration of the data.

Content analysis

Analytical approaches can also be conceptualized within the family of content analysis techniques. Content analysis is a procedure to track the multiplicity, variety, instability and historical contingency of the discursive constructions (Feltham-King & Macleod, 2016). Hsieh and Shannon (2005) suggest three approaches to content analysis: conventional, directed and summative.

While these approaches are similar, they differ from each other in the way coding data is performed. In the conventional content analysis, coding is developed directly from the data. Researchers read transcripts word-by-word, making notes, and developing codes, labels and categories. In directed content analysis, researchers follow a particular coding structure, guided by theory or a conceptual framework. It is mainly used to confirm, validate or extend a theory. While codes and categories are predefined, data that do not fit into a particular framework are often coded last. It is either treated as a subcategory or an emergent instance of a phenomenon. Summative content analysis is primarily concerned with the identification of keywords in text, how those words appear, who generates them and the usage and context in which the words appear. Analysis begins with reading the transcripts, familiarization and noting general ideas and generating initial codes. Once key concepts are identified, researchers can proceed to the development of a coding scheme.

Thematic analysis is another common method that draws from content analysis (Attride-Stirling, 2001). Again, it is a method for identifying and analyzing patterns of meaning in a dataset (Braun & Clarke, 2006; Bryman, 2006; Joffe, 2012)

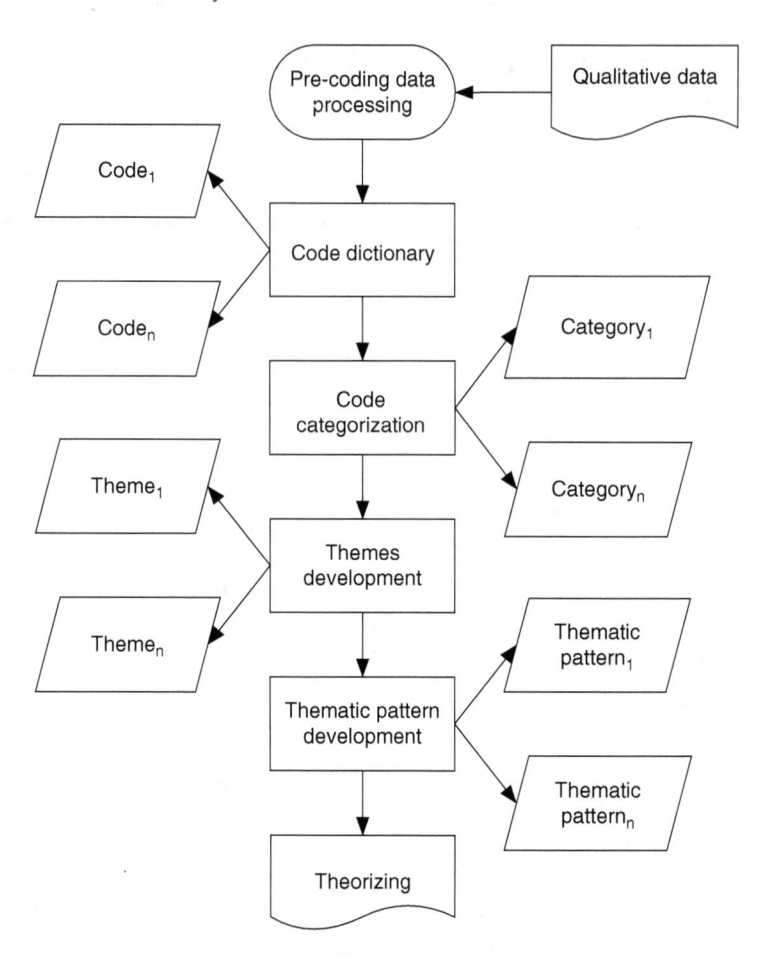

FIGURE 9.5 Thematic analysis of qualitative data

and the process is illustrated in Figure 9.5. Thematic analysis proceeds after the coding scheme is developed and involves the identification of themes through careful reading and re-reading of the data (Fereday & Muir-Cochrane, 2006; Rice & Ezzy, 1999). The outcome of a thematic analysis highlights the most noteworthy or interesting collections of meanings present in the dataset (Joffe, 2012).

In undertaking a thematic analysis, decisions need to be made about the process of identifying codes and themes, how similar codes are united to form certain categories, and how themes can be derived from codes. It also requires the researcher to develop a clear theoretical rationale for categorizing codes. Categories and a coding scheme can be derived from data, previous research or theories. When working on a research problem that has inadequate literature or theory, the researcher will need to generate categories from the data inductively. However, because thematic analysis always involves identification, analysis and discerning patterns within the data (Braun & Clarke, 2006), it shares much in common with all other analytical techniques. Two broad categories of thematic analysis are 'manifest' and 'latent' data analysis (also known as theory-driven and data-driven, respectively).

Manifest versus latent analysis

Manifest analysis is an intentional analysis of part of – or the entirety of – the dataset, aimed at understanding particular issues of interest. It requires researchers to sift through data and identify patterns using a predetermined criterion or set of criteria. In utilizing manifest data analysis, the researcher identifies and pre-categorizes participants or datasets according to some well-established theory. This procedure also requires pulling out key themes or issues with their frequencies and, if necessary, comparing results across meaningful categories. It is similar to deductive data analysis guided by a particular theoretical framework (Pope, Ziebland & Mays, 2000; Gale et al., 2013). The process is particularly useful in situations where the researcher is interested in testing a theory or in certain forms of comparative research.

In contrast, latent thematic analysis is driven by inductive approaches to knowledge or theory development. It is reductive in nature, as the researcher formulates a criterion for identifying themes based initially on the research question (Mayring & Fenzl, 2014). When performing an analysis, some categories in the coding scheme are obvious, and they can be drawn directly from the data. However, the categories are expected to be mutually exclusive (distinct from each other) and exhaustive. Analysts are likely to follow a grounded theory type of approach where the research does not derive categories from existing theories or previous related studies, but rather theory emerges from data (Thomas, 2006; Hsieh & Shannon, 2005). As discussed earlier, inductive analysis is highly relevant when there are no previous studies on the phenomenon or where the body of research in a particular area is multi-disciplinary or fragmented (Elo & Kyngäs, 2008).

Regardless of the approach taken, researchers need to consider either coding for occurrence or the prevalence in which a particular theme occurs within a single dataset or across participants represented in the data. A researcher might be interested in identifying whether there is a particular phenomenon within a dataset (occurrence) or counting the number of times such a phenomenon occurs (prevalence) within a single data point (individual transcript), or across data points (throughout all transcripts of data). The distinction between coding for prevalence alone, versus coding for prevalence and frequency, is an important one. Both need to be taken into account in determining thematic representation and acceptable levels of saturation in the observations.

Conclusion

Qualitative research analysis is an inquiry-based methodology for exploring, describing, explaining and understanding significant phenomenon. It is an epistemic enterprise, whereby the researcher interprets the meaning of data from what is observed. Observations are enriched by personal reflections and experiences, including knowledge of the subject and theory. While there are many analysis methods associated with qualitative research, Hsieh and Shannon (2005) suggest that all are similarly grounded in a series of steps, with the last step (evaluating the quality of findings) being the subject of Chapter 10:

1. Formulate a research question.
2. Select the sample to be analyzed.
3. Define categories to be applied to the data.
4. Develop and describe the coding process (content analysis-thematic analysis).
5. Develop codes or apply coding strategies to the data.
6. Evaluate the quality of findings.

Finally, no matter how structured or theoretically justified an analytical procedure is, it is only as good as the critical abilities of the person interpreting the data. It is possible to go through a highly structured process that gives the impression that a researcher is engaged in something objective or akin to pure science. Yet this is far from the case. Analytical procedures are helpful to follow but will not compensate in any project for lack of imagination and the capacity to develop new knowledge through an interaction between the data and published theory. In this context, we recommend two stages in the analysis, particularly for the novice. The first is very quick and involves developing all themes from the first reading of the data. This stage may be all that an expert requires. However, stage two involves adopting a more systematic approach, which gives time and opportunity for careful consideration of the data while developing factual and conceptual knowledge through continuing to engage in the literature. Preliminary themes may then change or be refined, but the two-stage process prevents the researcher getting bogged down in analysis for months at a time without seemingly making much progress.

Bibliography

Attride-Stirling, J. (2001). Thematic networks: An analytic tool for qualitative research, *Qualitative Research*, 1, 3: 385–405.

Auld, G.W., Diker, A., Bock, M.A., Boushey, C.J., Bruhn, C.M., Cluskey, M. & Reicks, M. (2007). Development of a decision tree to determine the appropriateness of NVivo in analyzing qualitative datasets, *Journal of Nutrition Education and Behavior*, 39, 1: 37–47.

Basit, T. (2003). Manual or electronic? The role of coding in qualitative data analysis, *Educational Research*, 45, 2: 143–154.

Braun, V. & Clarke, V. (2006). Using thematic analysis in psychology, *Qualitative Research in Psychology*, 3: 77–101.

Bryman, A. (2006). Integrating quantitative and qualitative research: How is it done? *Qualitative Research*, 6, 1: 97–113.

Cicchetti, D.V. (1976). Assessing inter-rater reliability for rating scales: Resolving some basic issues, *The British Journal of Psychiatry*, 129, 5: 452–456.
El Hussein, M., Jakubec, S.L. & Osuji, J. (2015). Assessing the FACTS: A mnemonic for teaching and learning the rapid assessment of rigor in qualitative research studies, *The Qualitative Report*, 20, 8: 1182–1184.
Elo, S. & Kyngäs, H. (2008). The qualitative content analysis process, *Journal of Advanced Nursing*, 62, 1: 107–115.
Feltham-King, T. & Macleod, C. (2016). How content analysis may complement and extend the insights of discourse analysis: An example of research on constructions of abortion in South African newspapers 1978–2005, *International Journal of Qualitative Methods*, 15, 1: 1–9.
Fereday, J. & Muir-Cochrane, E. (2006). Demonstrating rigor using thematic analysis: A hybrid approach of inductive and deductive coding and theme development, *International Journal of Qualitative Methods*, 5, 1: 80–92.
Gale, N.K., Heath, G., Cameron, E., Rashid, S. & Redwood, S. (2013). Using the framework method for the analysis of qualitative data in multi-disciplinary health research, *BMC Medical Research Methodology*, 13, 1: 117.
Gwet, K.L. (2014). *Handbook of inter-rater reliability: The definitive guide to measuring the extent of agreement among raters.* Gaithersburg, MD: Advanced Analytics, LLC.
Hartman, T. (2015). 'Strong multiplicity': An interpretive lens in the analysis of qualitative interview narratives, *Qualitative Research*, 15, 1: 22–38.
Hsieh, H.-F. & Shannon, S.E. (2005). Three approaches to qualitative content analysis, *Qualitative Health Research*, 15, 9: 1277–1288.
Joffe, H. (2012). Thematic analysis. In D. Harper & A.R. Thompson (Eds.), *Qualitative research methods in mental health and psychotherapy: A guide for students and practitioners* (pp. 210–223). Chichester, UK: Wiley-Blackwell.
Kamalodeen, V.J. & Jameson-Charles, M. (2016). A mixed methods research approach to exploring teacher participation in an online social networking website, *International Journal of Qualitative Methods*, 15, 1: 1–4.
Mayring, P. & Fenzl, T. (2014). Qualitative inhaltsanalyse. In *Handbuch Methoden der empirischen Sozialforschung* (pp. 543–556). Wiesbaden, Germany: Springer Fachmedien.
O'Dwyer, B. (2004). Qualitative data analysis: Illuminating a process for transforming a 'messy' but 'attractive' 'nuisance'. In C. Humphrey & B. Lee (Eds), *The real life guide to accounting research: A behind-the-scenes view of using qualitative research methods* (pp. 391–407). Oxford, UK: Elsevier Ltd.
Patton, M.Q. (2002). *Qualitative research and evaluation methods.* Thousand Oaks, CA: Sage.
Pope, C., Ziebland, S. & Mays, N. (2000). Analysing qualitative data, *British Medical Journal*, 320, 7227: 114–116.
Rice, P. & Ezzy, D. (1999). *Qualitative research methods: A health focus.* Melbourne, Australia: Oxford University Press.
Ritchie, J. & Spencer, L. (2002). Qualitative data analysis for applied policy research. In A.M. Huberman & M.B. Miles (Eds), *The qualitative researcher's companion* (pp. 305–329). Thousand Oaks, CA: Sage.
Ryan, J.J. & Ward, L.C. (1999). Validity, reliability, and standard errors of measurement for two seven-subtest short forms of the Wechsler Adult Intelligence Scale—III, *Psychological Assessment*, 11, 2: 207.
Schmid, H. (1981). The foundation: qualitative research and occupational therapy, *American Journal of Occupational Therapy*, 35, 2: 105.

Smith, J. & Firth, J. (2011). Qualitative data analysis: the framework approach, *Nurse Researcher*, 18, 2: 52–62.

Snelson, C.L. (2016). Qualitative and mixed methods social media research: A review of the literature, *International Journal of Qualitative Methods*, 15, 1: 1–15.

Thomas, D.R. (2006). A general inductive approach for analyzing qualitative evaluation data, *American Journal of Evaluation*, 27, 2: 237–246.

10
EVALUATING QUALITATIVE RESEARCH

Introduction

When a reader critiques a research article that has used a qualitative methodology, he or she should be asking a series of questions about the claims being made. This process is a necessary part of criticism that applies to all forms of research; however, qualitative studies present unique problems with respect to judging the research outcomes. These problems stem from qualitative studies having no simple methodological structure, rules or procedures to follow. Such structures are commonly found in quantitative methods and pure science, and this type of research is held in the highest esteem because of its perceived rigour, replicability, transferability and explanatory power. In contrast, qualitative research always carries a level of subjectivity and it is often only the concepts and theories that have some chance of being transferred to new situations. Even the idea of 'theory' in qualitative research can have many meanings (Chapter 6).

For some, the peculiarities of qualitative methodologies mean that these cannot be as valued as quantitative methodologies. One response to this position has been to apply quantitative criteria to qualitative frameworks, and by doing so, seek to increase the rigour and perceived worth of a study. This strategy uses the concepts of reliability and validity. However, these positivist ideas do not work well with many forms of qualitative work. For example, a narrative inquiry will be neither reliable nor valid, in the sense of reproducibility or accuracy of claims.

Rather than use reliability and validity, we present a framework based on four qualitative dimensions to guide decisions around evaluating qualitative research in higher education. The TACT framework is based on:

- (T)rustworthiness
- (A)uditability
- (C)redibility
- (T)ransferability

The development of the TACT framework has been informed by various discourses on 'rigour' that can be found in the research methods literature. To recap, qualitative methodology is concerned with exploring, describing, explaining and understanding the human condition. It is based on the analysis and interpretation of personal narratives and the lived experiences of participants (Sharts-Hopko, 2002). It has been called the second methodological tradition (Franklin, 1997) and numerous disciplines have employed qualitative research methods to address complex social problems.

Despite its growing contribution to methodological scholarship, the value of qualitative research studies has come under constant criticism (Ryan-Nicholls & Will, 2008; Myers, 2000). Critiques describe qualitative research as anecdotal, biased and limited in its power to generalize, since it only relies on detailed information about complex phenomena in one setting or context (Cope, 2014). In response to these growing criticisms, some methodologists have discussed various approaches for achieving a level of 'rigour' that will give the research certain qualities and so lift the standard of this type of work (Lietz, Langer & Furman, 2006; Hammersley, 1992; Guba & Lincoln, 1994; 1981). Rigour in this context is about thoroughness, precision and accuracy as fundamental conditions for trust in the research outcomes. Even this idea is contested and the body of research can be grouped into three broad categories:

1. The first category argues that the value of qualitative studies can be assessed using quantitative measures (e.g. reliability and validity) (see Tobin & Begley, 2004; Malterud, 2001). It is argued that: 'reliability and validity remain appropriate strategies for attaining rigor in qualitative research' (Morse et al., 2002, p. 13). Researchers in this category believe that reliability and validity can be applied to all research projects regardless of variations in paradigms or methods, since all research is concerned with findings that are plausible and applicable to other contexts (Hammersley, 1992; Kuzel & Engel, 2001; Morse et al., 2002). For example, studies in the health and behavioural sciences have used these quantitative approaches to assess the quality of qualitative research (Meyrick, 2006; Mays & Pope, 2000). Similarly, in the social sciences, Seale and Silverman (1997) proposed the use of objective measures. Critics of reliability and validity argue that social reality cannot be reduced to numerical approximations and instead the researcher should engage in establishing the 'authenticity' of research outcomes (Guba & Lincoln, 1989).

2. The second category proposes a set of criteria and standards based on interpretative ontologies (Rolfe, 2006; Shenton, 2004; Koch & Harrington, 1998; Baxter & Eyles, 1997). Attempts to develop interpretative paradigms for assessing rigour have led to the development of different terminologies and diverse conceptions of it (Morse, 1994). For example, Meyrick (2006) asks what 'good' qualitative research is and suggests that it should be judged on how 'transparent' and 'systematic' a study is. However, this author also asks irresolvable epistemological and ontological questions, such as how much transparency is required?

3   The third category questions the appropriateness of any general guidelines for evaluating qualitative research. This research suggests that universal standards for assessing qualitative methodologies are not needed. The rationale is that standards are unlikely to capture the complexity of individual projects and the web of relationships that evolve between the researcher, what is being researched and participants (Yardley, 2000; Leininger, 1994; Dixon-Woods et al., 2004). Further, it has been argued that developing a generic framework to assess the rigour of qualitative research would be inadequate because of the diversity of research paradigms (Popay et al., 1998; Barbour, 2001).

Despite differences in approaches to achieving some form of rigour in qualitative research, there is a consensus in the literature regarding its importance (Guba & Lincoln, 1981; Morse et al., 2002). With respect to this idea, we have developed a framework based on categories (1) and (2) above that we feel will be particularly useful to PhD students writing a qualitative higher education thesis, and for other qualitative researchers that require a way of claiming and justifying rigour in their work. The TACT framework (trustworthiness, auditability, credibility and transferability) (see Figure 10.1) brings together several different discourses around the importance of ensuring qualitative research is undertaken in a manner that enhances rigour. The overall intent of TACT is congruent with Koch's (2006) guidelines for evaluating the quality of qualitative studies and with Morse et al.'s (2002) view on the role rigour plays in enhancing research utility. The framework also has elements reflected in the work of Johnson et al. (2017).

The four main dimensions of the framework have a sub-set of categories that can be addressed systematically but all require subjective judgement with regards to whether or not these conditions have been met. In addition, some of the categories have similar purposes in more than one dimension and can thus be shared. The four dimensions are explained below:

1 Trustworthiness

Qualitative researchers are encouraged to achieve trustworthiness through the process of research as well as from the research outcomes. Trustworthiness enhances the reader's understanding and interpretation of findings, and enables them to establish a level of confidence in the quality of an investigation.

Sources and quality of data

Achieving trustworthiness requires a researcher to demonstrate that findings are situated within the views generated by participants (Lietz, Langer & Furman, 2006; Morrow, 2005; Sinkovics, Penz & Ghauri, 2008). Qualitative researchers need to show a systematic process for organizing and analyzing data (e.g. coding, identifying shared themes, categorizing themes), and a clear theoretical or logical rationale for eliminating overlapping themes (Creswell & Miller, 2000). Consistency in data

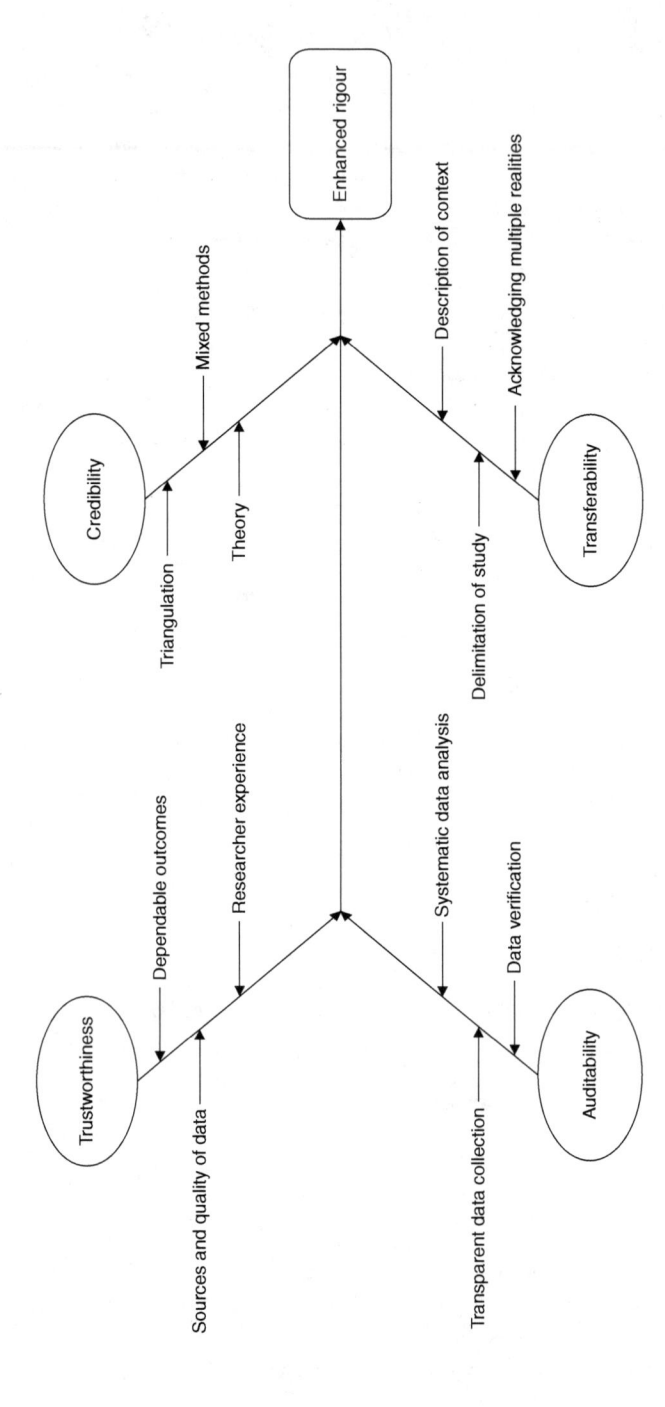

FIGURE 10.1 Dimensions of the TACT framework

analysis can also be achieved by determining intercoder reliability (Daniel, 2014; see Chapter 9).

Dependable outcomes

It is worth noting that establishing trustworthiness in qualitative research does not imply subscribing to a unified ontology, but rather demonstrating an acceptable degree of integrity in the process and outcome of the study. As Bailey (2007, p. 181) noted: 'trustworthiness does not mean that the reader necessarily has to agree with the researcher; rather it requires the reader to see how the researcher arrived at a conclusion'.

Researcher experience

A researcher needs to acknowledge personal biases and this may require a reflexive statement about research experience, explicitly establishing the distance between the researcher and the data (Seale & Silverman, 1997; Meyrick, 2006). Reflexivity requires a detailed account of experiences, assumptions about the phenomenon explored, and the process and circumstances that inform the data collection process. Krefting (1991) adds that the notion of neutrality is an important criterion for ensuring trustworthiness. Neutrality is the degree to which findings reflect participants' views outside of the researcher's biased opinions. Trustworthiness is also acquired when users can relate outcomes to their own experiences.

2 Auditability

Auditability requires the researcher to ensure that the research process is fully documented and described. It entails the provision of a record of all decisions made during the research process. Guba and Lincoln (1989, p. 243) termed this record checking procedure an 'audit trail'. An audit trail requires researchers to illustrate the evidence and thought processes that led to the conclusions in a study (Speziale & Carpenter, 2007). There are two types of auditability: external and internal. External auditability is typically carried out by research users, including PhD examiners, especially when findings or conclusions appear to be suspect (Morse, 2015). In contrast, internal auditability relates to the ability of the researcher to address methodological issues. For example, stating a research question clearly and then aligning it with a particular research design, the data analysis and conclusions drawn (Halpern, 1983).

Transparent data collection

Details of an audit trail in a methods section need to be sufficiently explained to make it possible for other researchers to understand how an inquiry has been undertaken. The quality of this account can be judged by the extent to which others can learn from the process.

Systematic data analysis

The analysis itself must be seen as systematic and well justified. In research that relies on interviews, quotations to illustrate concepts are important. In addition, field notes, memos and pictures can be used to help researchers to justify claims.

Data verification

Data verification is usually associated with quantitative methods but the verification principle of checking for accuracy can apply equally to qualitative research. In addition, when more than one type of data are used in a study, these can be cross-checked in the process of triangulation (see below).

3 Credibility

The notion of credibility in qualitative research is similar to internal validity in quantitative research, but in this case it is an approximation of some truth. Credibility requires establishing that findings are credible, relevant and congruent. These conditions take into account the position that the perspectives of those who provided the data can influence researchers (Sandelowski, 1986; Patton, 1999). Credibility can be achieved through a careful description of data collection through verification of the sources from which the data is obtained, and through a description of the analysis. It also requires researchers to anchor the unit of data analysis in the central phenomenon being investigated.

Triangulation

Triangulation relates to the convergence of data interpretations obtained from two or more data sources. It is also used to substantiate partial findings from one type of data through another. To achieve credibility in this way, Creswell (2009) advises researchers return the final report to the participants for verification purposes. This process is also referred to as 'member checking' (Loh, 2013; Morse, 2015).

Mixed method

We do not categorize mixed methods research as a separate paradigm, although it is commonly used to answer research questions with two or more methods from quantitative and/or qualitative research traditions. Typical examples in higher education are interviews with either focus groups or surveys. Mixed methods are not a condition of credibility but can certainly contribute to it. If similar conclusions are reached from both methods, or if one supports the other, then this can augment the credibility of claims. However, mixed methods also tend to give the *impression* that the research is credible and so care must be taken in evaluation.

Theory

Theory (Chapter 8) use is always a central part of any judgement about the quality of research. When a theoretical perspective is used for a study, the results should connect to and contribute to it. The same argument applies when results drawn from existing theory, or theories, are used to justify conclusions.

4 Transferability

Transferability in qualitative research is congruent to the concept of reliability in quantitative methodology. In contrast to quantitative epistemology, however, transferability does not advocate for generalizability, but instead suggests that findings gained in a particular context can offer valuable lessons for other similar settings.

Delimitation of study

This is about the choices a researcher has made in the study that make clear what has been included and why this has been done, as well as explaining what has been excluded.

Description of content

Numerous studies state that transferability is a type of external validity achieved by describing a phenomenon in sufficient detail (Myers, 1997; Lincoln & Guba, 1985; Golafshani, 2003). Lincoln and Guba (1985) mentioned that transferability occurs when a researcher provides enough details about the context of the study and sufficient information to enable others to make a comparison and decide whether the environment in which a particular research is conducted is similar to other settings of interest (Shenton, 2004).

Acknowledgement of multiple realities

Findings of a study must first accurately reflect the views of those who participated in the study. As such, the researcher has to accept multiple realities, work with them in the analysis and present them in the final account (Golafshani, 2003; Myers, 1997). In addition, readers will have their own take on what the writer presents and so a researcher will never know for sure how the results have been interpreted.

Conclusion

From a methodological point of view, the quality of research needs to be checked against the soundness of problem formulation, research design, theoretical depth, methods for data collection, analytical rigour and the conclusions drawn. The TACT framework for determining rigour in qualitative research helps guide the

> Results from an empirical verification of the TACT framework suggest that postgraduate students and academics found it useful for learning about rigour in qualitative research methods. TACT also served as an important theoretical tool for initiating further discourses on aspects of rigour in qualitative research methodology.
>
> In brief, the investigation used a survey instrument that was first piloted and tested for reliability revealing a Cronbach's Alpha ($\alpha = 0.86$) indicating a good level of internal consistency (George & Mallery, 2003). One hundred and thirty participants who were taught the TACT framework responded. They were mainly postgraduates from different disciplines. Respondents rated each statement on the scale and responded to open-ended questions that were subsequently analyzed thematically. This analysis involved reading and re-reading responses to gain familiarization with the text, developing codes and then grouping codes into themes. Results showed that the TACT generic framework provided a valuable teaching toolkit. Overall, participants found TACT to be a useful tool for learning how to evaluate research. The use of theoretical indicators provided an understanding of transferability, legitimacy and the need to gain trust from those interested in using their research.
>
> Two survey comments were:
>
> TACT will be useful for qualitative researchers because it facilitates transparency, reliability and trustworthiness of the data collected throughout the research process.
>
> (Respondent 1)
>
> Qualitative researchers need to be able to reveal the validity and the reliability of their study. For that, they need an assessment with adequate information and theoretical underpinning. The researcher should open up the avenues for the future researchers by stating the limitations of the present study.
>
> (Respondent 2)

FIGURE 10.2 Testing the TACT framework

evaluation of a study, particularly in determining its theoretical accuracy. In addition, if there is a commitment to establishing rigour from the start, it can make researchers accountable during the research process. Preliminary empirical verification of the value of TACT suggests that emerging researchers found TACT to be a useful framework and a toolkit for learning about the concept of rigour (see Figure 10.2). However, what constitutes 'rigour' will remain open to interpretation.

With different methodological traditions addressing the complex problems of higher education, researchers familiar with science and positivist paradigms tend to seek similar rules and procedures for ensuring quality. However, shared criteria for judging work (or criteria that have shared meanings) are not available in qualitative work. The TACT framework takes a step in this direction but also serves to open up debate on the complex challenge of providing general standards for those who wish to evaluate qualitative studies. We suggest that TACT is particularly useful for improving the quality of one's own research and can be used as a guide for those tasked with reviewing a research paper or examining a thesis.

Bibliography

Bailey, C.A. (2007). *A guide to qualitative field research* (2nd ed). Thousand Oaks, CA: Pine Forge Press.

Barbour, R.S. (2001). Checklists for improving rigour in qualitative research: A case of the tail wagging the dog? *British Medical Journal*, 322, 7294: 1133–7448.

Baxter, J. & Eyles, J. (1997). Evaluating qualitative research in social geography: Establishing 'rigour' in interview analysis, *Transactions of the Institute of British Geographers*, 22, 4: 505–525.

Cope, D.G. (2014). Methods and meanings: Credibility and trustworthiness of qualitative research, *In Oncology Nursing Forum*, 41, 1: 89–91.

Creswell, J.W. (2009). Editorial, *Mapping the Field of Mixed Methods Research*, 3, 2: 95–108.

Creswell, J.W. & Miller, D.L. (2000). Determining validity in qualitative inquiry, *Theory into Practice*, 3, 3: 124–130.

Daniel, B.K. (2014). A research methodology for studying distributed communities of practice, *International Journal of Web Based Communities*, 10, 4: 506–516. doi: 10.1504/IJWBC.2014.065397

Dixon-Woods, M., Shaw, R.L., Agarwal, S. & Smith, J.A. (2004). The problem of appraising qualitative research, *Quality and Safety in Health Care*, 13, 3: 223–225.

Franklin, C. (1997). Learning to teach qualitative research: Reflections of a quantitative researcher, *Marriage & Family Review*, 24, 4: 241–274.

George, D. & Mallery, M. (2003). *Using SPSS for Windows step by step: A simple guide and reference* (4th ed). Boston, MA: Allyn & Bacon.

Golafshani, N. (2003). Understanding reliability and validity in qualitative research, *The Qualitative Report*, 8, 4: 597–606.

Guba, E.G. & Lincoln, Y.S. (1981). *Effective evaluation: Improving the usefulness of evaluation results through responsive and naturalistic approaches*. San Francisco, CA: Jossey-Bass Publishers.

Guba, E.G. & Lincoln, Y.S. (1989). *Fourth generation evaluation*. London, UK: Sage Publications.

Guba, E.G. & Lincoln, Y.S. (1994). Competing paradigms in qualitative research. In Denzin, N.K. & Lincoln, Y.S. (Eds), *Handbook of qualitative research* (pp. 163–194). Thousand Oaks, CA: Sage Publications.

Halpern, E.S. (1983) Auditing naturalistic inquiries: The development and application of a model (doctoral dissertation). Indiana University, IN.

Hammersley, M. (1992). By what criteria should ethnographic research be judged? In *What's wrong with ethnography?* (pp. 57–82). Abingdon, UK: Routledge.

Johnston, C.M., Wallis, M., Oprescu, F.I. & Gray, M. (2017). Methodological considerations related to nurse researchers using their own experience of a phenomenon within phenomenology, *Journal of Advanced Nursing*, 73, 3: 574–584.

Koch, T. (2006). Establishing rigour in qualitative research: The decision trail, *Journal of Advanced Nursing*, 53, 1: 91–100.

Koch, T. & Harrington, A. (1998). Reconceptualizing rigour: The case for reflexivity, *Journal of Advanced Nursing*, 28, 4: 882–890.

Krefting, L. (1991). Rigor in qualitative research: The assessment of trustworthiness, *American Journal of Occupational Therapy*, 45, 3: 214–222.

Kuzel, A.J. & Engel, J.D. (2001). Some pragmatic thoughts about evaluating qualitative health research: The nature of qualitative evidence. In J. Morse, J. Swanson & A. Kuzel (Eds), *The nature of qualitative evidence* (pp. 114–138). Thousand Oaks, CA: Sage.

Leininger, M. (1994). Evaluation criteria and critique of qualitative research studies. In J.M. Morse (Ed.), *Critical issues in qualitative research methods* (pp. 95–115). London, UK: Sage Publications.

Lietz, C.A., Langer, C.L. & Furman, R. (2006). Establishing trustworthiness in qualitative research in social work: Implications from a study regarding spirituality, *Qualitative Social Work*, 5, 4: 441–458.

Lincoln, Y.S. & Guba, E.G. (1985). *Naturalistic inquiry*. Thousand Oaks, CA: Sage.

Loh, J. (2013). Inquiry into issues of trustworthiness and quality in narrative studies: A perspective, *The Qualitative Report*, 18, 3: 1–15. Retrieved 13 September 2017 from nsuworks.nova.edu/tqr/vol18/iss33/1/

Malterud, K. (2001). Qualitative research: Standards, challenges, and guidelines, *The Lancet*, 358, 9280: 483–488.

Mays, N. & Pope, C. (2000). Assessing quality in qualitative research, *British Medical Journal*, 320, 7226: 50.

Meyrick, J. (2006). What is good qualitative research? A first step towards a comprehensive approach to judging rigour/quality, *Journal of Health Psychology*, 11, 5: 799–808.

Morrow, S.L. (2005). Quality and trustworthiness in qualitative research in counseling psychology, *Journal of Counseling Psychology*, 52, 2: 250.

Morse, J.M. (Ed.) (1994). *Critical issues in qualitative research methods*. London, UK: Sage Publications.

Morse, J.M. (2015). Critical analysis of strategies for determining rigor in qualitative inquiry, *Qualitative Health Research*, 25, 9: 1212–1222.

Morse, J.M., Barrett, M., Mayan, M., Olson, K. & Spiers, J. (2002). Verification strategies for establishing reliability and validity in qualitative research, *International Journal of Qualitative Methods*, 1, 2: 13–22.

Myers, M. (1997). Qualitative research in information systems, *Management Information Systems Quarterly*, 21, 2: 241–242.

Myers, M. (2000). Qualitative research and the generalizability question: Standing firm with Proteus, *The Qualitative Report*, 4, 3: 1–14.

Patton, M.Q. (1999). Enhancing the quality and credibility of qualitative analysis, *Health Services Research*, 34, 5: 1189–1208.

Popay, J., Rogers, A., & Williams, G. (1998). Rationale and standards for the systematic review of qualitative literature in health services research, *Qualitative Health Research*, 8, 3: 341–351.

Rolfe, G. (2006). Validity, trustworthiness, and rigour: Quality and the idea of qualitative research, *Journal of Advanced Nursing*, 53, 3: 304–310.

Ryan-Nicholls, K. & Will, C. (2008). Rigour in qualitative research: Mechanisms for control, *Nurse Researcher*, 16, 3: 70–85.

Sandelowski, M. (1986). The problem of rigor in qualitative research, *Advances in Nursing Science*, 8, 3: 27–37.

Seale, C. & Silverman, D. (1997). Ensuring rigour in qualitative research, *The European Journal of Public Health*, 7, 4: 379–384.

Sharts-Hopko, N.C. (2002). Assessing rigor in qualitative research, *Journal of the Association of Nurses in AIDS Care*, 13, 4: 84–86.

Shenton, A.K. (2004). Strategies for ensuring trustworthiness in qualitative research projects, *Education for Information*, 22, 2: 63–75.

Sinkovics, R.R., Penz, E. & Ghauri, P.N. (2008). Enhancing the trustworthiness of qualitative research in international business, *Management International Review*, 48, 6: 689–714.

Speziale, H.J.S. & Carpenter, D.R. (2007). The conduct of qualitative research: Common essential elements. In *Qualitative research in nursing: Advancing the humanistic imperative* (pp. 19–33). Philadelphia, PA: Lippincott.

Tobin, G.A. & Begley, C.M. (2004). Methodological rigour within a qualitative framework, *Journal of Advanced Nursing*, 48, 4: 388–396.

Tong, A., Flemming, K., McInnes, E., Oliver, S. & Craig, J. (2012). Enhancing transparency in reporting the synthesis of qualitative research: ENTREQ, *BMC Medical Research Methodology*, 12, 1. Retrieved 13 September 2017, from www.biomedcentral.com/1471-2288/12/181

Yardley, L. (2000). Dilemmas in qualitative health research, *Psychology and Health*, 15, 2: 215–228.

11
WRITING FOR PUBLICATION

Introduction

The object of learning about research methods is to enable the beginning or experienced researcher to better understand how to approach their research project and perhaps come to some new appreciation of the possibilities for research design. In the study of higher education, like all research, the starting point is a good question to frame the inquiry and this can be overlooked in the quest for the perfect method and study design.

We have seen new researchers become narrowly focused on the 'how to' while losing sight of the question. Theoretically, a question should determine the methods and sources in qualitative or mixed methods research but we suggest that this alignment only partially represents what happens in practice (Bryman, 2007). In addition, when using qualitative research paradigms that focus on 'discovery', a research question usually evolves and changes during the study when ideas emerge from the data that take the researcher's thinking in a new direction. As such, the researcher should always be prepared to re-visit the question during or at the end of a study and see if it is still the most appropriate one to ask. It may have to be modified, or re-written, but a question, even an evolving one, should always direct the researcher or research team.

Like many higher education researchers, the authors of this book tend to work with certain methods for which we have developed expertise, but we also have an interest in methodology itself. This interest will sometimes push us to try a new approach or method out of curiosity and then retrospectively see how well it helped to answer the question. Through trial and error (rather than any theoretical certainty or alignment) we have learned that the outcome is always that the new method 'partially' answers the question and that it usually produces surprises that contribute to the research in unforeseen ways. Yet again, this approach reflects the transformational potential of discovery research and may lead to modifying the original question.

The next proposition is embryonic but worth considering. If the research question is constantly brought to mind, either to guide the research project, or to check if it is still relevant, then this will influence each step of the research process. The question has a role in directing the quality of thinking around the subject itself, and so contributes to how the research might lead to new knowledge that can make a contribution a) to the field and b) to practice. This outcome has to be the ultimate purpose of any research and our shared ontology is firmly grounded in a belief that research in the subject of higher education should be both knowledge-focused and practical. The link between these goals may not be concurrent or even direct. In a similar way, some blue-skies science discoveries only later find an application, or enhance theory formation. We hypothesize that seeking application or a new theory in the design of a project while relentlessly reflecting on the (set or emerging) research question will impact on the quality of the work and how it will eventually be judged.

With respect to producing a worthwhile research question in the first place, the PhD or master's student should be well supported, because it is unlikely that a supervisor or supervisory team would allow old or established work to be repeated, and if they are up-to-date in their field, they will have a fair idea of what needs to or can be done. In addition, the PhD student has three years or more in which to focus on the question, a long period and a luxury that the pressured academic seldom has in today's performative higher education. As shown in Chapter 2, most published higher education research is in the form of empirical case studies or is conceptual in nature. Both forms require a good question and if this is the starting point, the work should be capable of producing research that has something to say, and so make a contribution to the field.

1 Mind the gap

Novice researchers in higher education, and other forms of social or humanities research, are often advised to look for a 'gap' in knowledge that the researcher can 'fill' with a project. The problem with this idea is that there are limitless gaps in knowledge, either in pure science or in our understanding of human experiences. In the same way, there are limitless problems to address through research. However, not all problems or gaps are equal and good research progresses through choosing the 'right' gap. In any thesis, journal article or grant application, those who judge it will not be interested in gap statements but in a clear exposition of why the research is important. The fact that we do not know something is not a justification for doing research. Successful researchers mind the gap but judge very carefully what is important and what will make the most significant contribution to knowledge. A test has been suggested when choosing a research topic (Jones, 2003). This requires an answer to the following questions:

1   Who cares?
2   So what?

The first deals with relevance and interest; the second with the implications of your research. The PhD student or novice will find it difficult to provide answers for themselves. In fact, even experts can have doubts about the importance of their work. In all cases, it is wise to seek candid answers to these questions from supervisors or more experienced researchers.

2 A systematic inquiry made public

As previously stated in the Introduction and Chapter 7, Lawrence Stenhouse (1981) described research as a 'systematic inquiry made public'. This rather brief and elegant definition is worth repeating because it combines the project design (a systematic inquiry) with what we would suggest is an ultimate and necessary goal for research (making it public). If anyone completes a research project, writes it up, puts it in a locked cupboard and never talks about it again, then it is not research. To be research, the work must be made public and it is very important not to lose sight of this. It allows you to claim being a researcher, but it also determines the quality of thinking, because the quest for publication changes the nature and quality of thought. We have all met very clever academics whose ideas don't travel far because they do not publish them in written form for a wider audience. If the idea is good, then get it out in the public domain.

Of course there are many ways of making research public and each is likely to have a different impact on the research process. Typical modes are giving a seminar, presenting at a conference or writing a thesis, a book, a book chapter or journal article. Each of these modes changes the way we think and shape how knowledge is constructed. From a cultural point of view, there seems to be a hierarchy of publication types and, at each level, there is more at stake and so more motivation and pressure to produce something of greater quality. The peer reviewed journal article remains supreme, despite many recent changes in publication types. Figure 11.1 illustrates this hierarchy (Harland, 2012). A systematic inquiry becomes research when the outcomes are in the public domain. Typical examples are action research (AR), the Scholarship of Teaching and Learning (SoTL) and shared accounts of reflective practice (RP). Once we reach the stage of research seminars and journal articles, we enter the domain of higher education (HE) as a field of research.

There is much more at stake when we present our work to an expert audience than when we share our thoughts with a supervisor or colleague, especially when the work is the subject of review and criticism. There is also a different level of precision and argument required when a conference presentation is compared to a peer reviewed journal article. Conferences are often used to test ideas and you will find consistent advice across the field not to write a full conference paper if your work is good enough for a journal. When books and book chapters are considered, much will depend on the rigour of the peer review process and the reputation of the publishing house.

The higher education journal article tends to be the pinnacle research outlet and we would even say that it can have more impact than much larger works, such

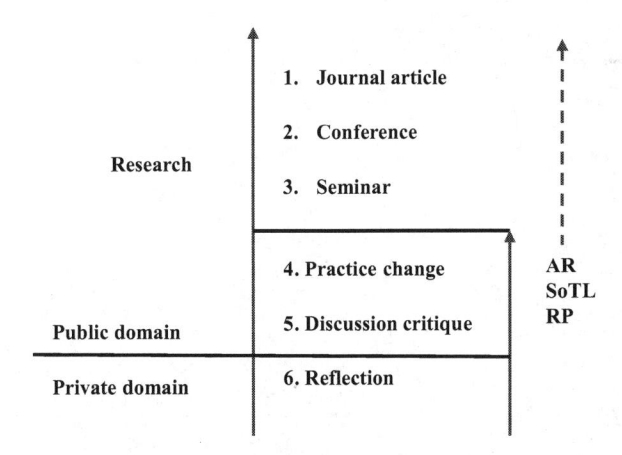

```
                                1. Journal article
                                2. Conference
            Research
                                3. Seminar

                                4. Practice change      AR
                                                        SoTL
            Public domain       5. Discussion critique  RP

            Private domain      6. Reflection
```

FIGURE 11.1 Forms of systematic inquiry

as an original book or edited volume. Journal articles tend to be more widely read than books and reach a bigger audience. This argument, partly based on evidence from citations, does not always hold and it is possible to find, for example, books that have huge citation numbers (e.g. Biggs and Tang's (2007) book on university teaching had 12,607 at the time of writing this chapter). However, our advice is to aim for the best peer reviewed higher education journal possible and the research account will likely to be subject to the most rigorous peer review process you can experience. Although peer review has been highly criticized, it will generally lift the quality of the final paper, even if the outcome is revision or rejection. Much can be learned about the quality of the work for journal reviewers and it is a good idea to ask peers to read the work before submission.

3 The problems with submitted work

In 2014, an analysis was carried out on the journal refereeing reports that had been completed by one of the authors of this book. These reports had been kept on file and were examined with the objective of seeking patterns in why a recommendation to accept, reject or revise had been made for each submitted research paper. These refereeing reports had been commissioned by many of the major higher education journals listed in the Web of Knowledge ISI rankings database. Although one could argue that such a sample is one referee's opinion (N=1), journals often share reports to let a referee know what the other referee(s) have been thinking, and this gives some confidence that a decision has been the correct one. However, it must be noted that a shared decision may have arisen for quite different reasons.

In this analysis, 161 rejected refereeing reports (written between 2002 and 2014) were read with the following question in mind: 'What are the main reasons for rejecting research articles submitted to a journal?' The results are shown in Table 11.1.

TABLE 11.1 Why 161 articles were rejected after submission to a higher education journal

Rank order*	Problem	Explanation
1	Research article is inconsequential (applied, theoretical or conceptual)	• Very little to add to what is already known (or to the debate) • Does not develop new ideas • Implications weak • Unlikely others will learn from it
2	Lack of integration	• Does not engage critically with what's out there and makes poor use of theory • Is not written to contribute to theory or a field of practice
3	Poor use of evidence	• There is a big enough gap between claims and evidence to raise concerns • History of ideas ignored
4	Sections are not aligned	• Literature review route rather than background to research question and findings
5	Grammar and meaning	• Finding it hard to express ideas and poor use of English

* Rank shows order of importance (frequency) but most rejected articles had a number of problems.

The results of this exercise were more complicated than first envisaged. Although the themes presented in Table 11.1 are ranked in order of importance, none were mutually exclusive and no articles were rejected on the basis of 4 and 5 alone. Both 'Sections are not aligned' and 'Grammar and meaning' tended to contribute to the final review decision but on their own would not have resulted in rejection. Researchers, however, should be very sure of the quality of their submission if they want to have the best chance of publication. Our advice is to use peers in a department or a similar field to review the article before it is offered to a journal.

Papers that get straight acceptances tend to show the converse of the rejection categories. Yet our view is that if a manuscript has problems but has something to say (e.g. rank 1) we would always provide substantial guidance and encouragement for revision and move from an emphasis on 'gatekeeper' to 'mentor'. In turn, when our own work has been judged in a similar manner, we have both had tremendous support from anonymous referees. This value commitment seems to bring out the best in the peer review process.

At the same time, peer review is not perfect and the process has been subject to much criticism. We have both lost out and had rejections for what we regarded as strong papers. However, on each occasion rejection has resulted in a revised article being much clearer and with arguments that are more convincing, before submitting to a new journal. Acceptance and rejection are just part of the rhythm of research life. It is, however, hard for the new researcher to accept this situation and publishing can be an emotional roller coaster and at times feel like a lottery. Subjective judgement and poor refereeing is part of the qualitative higher education research landscape.

If we take the main reason for rejection from the analysis, that the research has little to add to what is already known, this in itself does not mean the research will not be published. There are millions of inconsequential research articles out there if we simply judge significance by citations evidence. Your own reading will certainly confirm this observation but this situation should never give hope. When we read in the vast literature on higher education, we find 'repeated' research with similar conclusions. Each case will never be exactly the same because of context, but the differences are not enough to allow new theory to be developed. Type in 'problem based learning' into Google Scholar and you will find 3.59 million results of one type or other (July 2017). They cannot all have something unique to say. A good research article will clearly show a critical approach to theory choice, knowledge construction and the claims made.

On the other hand, the idea of integration with 'what's out there' is very important. There is an incredibly rich history of ideas that we can build on and higher education, like all social forms of research, is inherently multidisciplinary with knowledge that is seemingly endless and expanding. These circumstances partially explain why PhD students find it hard to deal with the perceived lack of boundaries as they read for their research. When to stop reading is a widespread problem for the new researcher. Experienced academics might see their work as finished and ready to submit when they:

1 are sure they can make a contribution;
2 have exhausted their ideas; and
3 feel that they can go no further at this point in time.

(Jones, 2003)

Note that neither of us has rejected a journal article because the methods have been flawed or poorly written. The methods might not be explained well, or may not be aligned with the analysis and results, but generally they have been relevant to the research question and were, at the very least, adequate. It can all be fixed relatively easily. This situation suggests that once learned, research methods can be approached technically and then a researcher's job becomes one of improving their methodological skills. However, methodological change should also come through ontological and epistemological development or by challenging orthodoxy to see what new methods might emerge.

Conclusion

We have included these ideas on writing and publication because we know from experience that these subjects occupy the mind of all those learning about research methods. Quality research comes from deep intellectual engagement and pursuing relevant questions. There are endless questions to ask but successful researchers can see which are the most important to seek answers to, or perhaps tend to be lucky in their choice. Over time, probability will ensure that luck will run out, so learn to focus on what is worth asking. To answer the question: 'What is worthwhile doing in research?' is about value judgement that must relate to what the researcher or research team considers the purposes of higher education. This idea is explored in Chapter 12.

Bibliography

Biggs, J. & Tang, C. (2007). *Teaching for quality at university*. Maidenhead, UK: McGraw Hill and Open University Press.

Bryman, A. (2007). The research question in social research: What is its role? *International Journal of Social Research Methodology*, 10, 1: 5–20.

Harland, T. (2012). *University teaching: An introductory guide*. London, UK: Routledge.

Jones, R. (2003). Choosing a research question, *Asia Pacific Family Medicine*, 2: 42–44.

Stenhouse, L. (1981). What counts as research? *British Journal of Educational Studies*, 14, 2: 103–114.

12
FINAL WORDS

For those wishing to study any discipline, methodological understanding is part of the process. Even those studying a subject without taking part in research require a certain level of insight into methodology to be able to judge the worth of arguments, claims and conclusions. To do this requires both epistemic access to the procedures of knowledge creation and a disposition of mind that has certain qualities that are often hard to define. These might be described by words such as creative, critical and insightful. The qualities are obvious and impressive when we see them displayed by a researcher or a critic, and it could be argued that they are always present in the best research published in a subject. This argument is really self-evident and we know from teaching and supervising students and mentoring new researchers that quality of thought is *the* major concern for the learner. There is much less anxiety about understanding and implementing research methodology even though this is often a slow process. What students want most guidance on is how to make a powerful argument, how to critique data, how to integrate ideas from different disciplines, and how to come up with something both original and worthwhile. The idea of 'making a contribution' is quite strong in higher education research because of its pragmatic foundations and applied character.

Of course, no one starts out in life as creative and critical and these dispositions or qualities need to be learned. For research, this will be in the context of a strong theoretical disciplinary framework. Starting with a systematic exploration of methodology will contribute to the quality of thought, and the technical aspects of conducting a competent study provide a framework on which to hang original ideas and create something new. With experience, these two aspects meld into one practice and so competence in qualitative methods, for example, becomes intuitive or procedural and so leaves more time to focus on originality and making the best contribution possible. This task requires deliberative thinking about the work itself and can be achieved in the process of analysis and writing and/or after the first draft of the study. Revisiting ideas essentially extends the analysis but however a conclusion is reached, the quality goal is always the same.

In one sense, learning higher education methodologies is about getting the basics right and this is important for both novices and experts. In the book, we have made suggestions about what we think are the essential components of both the research process and the final written product. We can write about and teach these ideas with some confidence and know that they can be learned. What is much more difficult to teach is imaginative thinking. It could be argued that discovering a new fact has intrinsic value, but there are few genuinely new things to be discovered in the social world we study and, even if this were the case, they will still have to be sold to others in a burgeoning marketplace of ideas.

Like most things, learning to be a good researcher can be described as a 'journey'. This ubiquitous metaphor needs wheeling out and repeating again and again for our students. Those who study higher education with us (and this is probably the situation in most other subjects) want quick success and there is little tolerance in either the university or society more broadly for the long-term gestation of ideas, or reward for the culmination of a lifetime's work. Every activity seems to be reduced to the minimum time possible and is often measured by others to re-enforce this value through compliance. Higher education is particularly susceptible to outside pressures. Our students, for example, want to succeed quickly ('get some publishing success under their belt'). Although the PhD thesis is traditionally written within a set period, we now have students wishing to emulate recent practices in science by trying to write a qualitative thesis as a series of research articles. The goal is to have these articles published before thesis submission. Our view is that we need to support such ambitions where possible, but experience has shown that most higher education students will not be able to publish in a journal after a matter of weeks into their apprenticeship without considerable input from more experienced researchers. Usually we would only support this way of doing a PhD if the discipline of writing the paper then influenced the quality of the rest of the thesis and did not prolong the PhD period.

However, it is not just PhD students who want quick success in publishing within a short time of entering the higher education field. Colleagues from many other disciplines have come to work with us and some have the expectation that only a short time is required to produce work of international significance. These academics may feel the study of higher education is easy compared to their first discipline. (For example, who could come into astrophysics and publish in an international journal after a few weeks of study? What would the astrophysicist say to me if I suggested I could do this?) Yet this is our situation and working with academics from other disciplines is a valued part of our culture. We know that these scholars can bring skills in research, critical abilities, talent and intellect that have all been acquired from years of experience in their first discipline, and then apply these to higher education research. In addition, academics often research into the teaching of their first discipline, and so also have some relevant subject knowledge and practical experience. They also tend to pick up the more complex and difficult methodological ideas faster than the true novice PhD student. We argue that some parts of the research process often take longer than they should for the new researcher and can be traversed a lot quicker with the right guidance. Here we include most parts of methodology. Swiftly getting to grips with, for example, approaches, methods and initial analysis, should free up time for reading and thinking about the more conceptual and creative parts of the research project.

A good idea can be incubated over a number of years and may need to be pursued relentlessly until gestation is complete and it is ready to be shared with the world. In our experience, deliberative thinking and the pursuit of ideas always involve our colleagues and students in critical dialogue. We may like to think of ourselves as 'driven' in the pursuit of knowledge, and if this picture of determination and single-mindedness reflects a measure of success (no matter how pretentious or grandiose this claim seems), then can the same be asked of the novice or even developed through experience? This essential principle for success is very complicated. Students need to take ownership of their own research area and possession includes a love of subject and a passion for discovering new things. Being interested and passionate is not always apparent in the new researcher and appears absent when a thesis student becomes fed up with what they are doing. We hope that our book will not only help to instill passion, curiosity and tenacity, but make it easier and quicker to navigate higher education methodology and take away a common flat spot on the research journey. In this way, students can spend more time focusing on the more challenging aspects of research and quality of thought and in doing so make a worthwhile contribution to knowledge.

FURTHER READING

We have compiled a list of further readings that we find ourselves referring to often. Some of these references also appear in the text in some chapters.

General references on research methodology

Creswell, J.W. (1994). *Research design: Qualitative and quantitative approaches*. Thousand Oaks, CA: Sage.
Creswell, J.W. (2009). *Designing a qualitative study: Qualitative, quantitative and mixed methods approaches* (3rd ed). Thousand Oaks, CA: Sage.
Creswell, J.W. (2013). *Research design: Qualitative, quantitative, and mixed methods approaches*. Thousand Oaks, CA: Sage.
Maykut, P., Maykut, P.S. & Morehouse, R. (1994). *Beginning qualitative research: A philosophic and practical guide* (vol. 6). London, UK: Psychology Press.
Patton, M.Q. (2002). *Qualitative research and evaluation methods*. Thousand Oaks, CA: Sage.

Chapter 1 The study of higher education

Barnett, R. (2000). *Realizing the university in an age of supercomplexity*. Buckingham, UK: The Society for Research into Higher Education & Open University Press.
Boyer, E.L. (1990). *Scholarship reconsidered: Priorities of the professoriate*. Princeton, NJ: The Carnegie Foundation for the Advancement of Teaching.
Dewey, J. (1916). *Democracy and education*. New York, NY: The MacMillan Company.
Harland, T. (2009). People who study higher education, *Teaching in Higher Education*, 14, 5: 579–582.
Harland, T. (2012). Higher education as an open-access discipline, *Higher Education Research & Development*, 31, 5: 703–710.
Rowland, S. (2006). *The enquiring university: Compliance and contestation in higher education*. Buckingham, UK: Open University Press/McGraw-Hill Education. Higher Education Research & Development.

Tight, M. (2003). *Researching higher education*. Maidenhead, UK: The Society for Research in Higher Education and Open University Press.

Chapter 2 Ontology and epistemology

Bryman, A. (1992). *Quantity and quality in social research*. London, UK: Routledge.
de Gialdino, I.V. (2009). Ontological and epistemological foundations of qualitative research, *Forum Qualitative Sozialforschung/Forum: Qualitative Social Research*, 10, 2.
Guba, E.G. (1990). The alternative paradigm dialog. In E.G. Guba (Ed), *The paradigm dialog* (pp. 17–30). Thousand Oaks, CA: Sage.
Scotland, J. (2012). Exploring the philosophical underpinnings of research: Relating ontology and epistemology to the methodology and methods of the scientific, interpretive, and critical research paradigms, *English Language Teaching*, 5, 9: 9.

Chapter 3 Qualitative research approaches

Bochner, A.P. (2012). On first person narrative scholarship: Autoethnography as acts of meaning, *Narrative Inquiry*, 22, 1: 155–164.
Clegg, S. & Stevenson, J. (2013). The interview reconsidered: Context, genre, reflexivity and interpretation in sociological approaches to interviews in higher education research, *Higher Education Research and Development*, 32, 1: 5–16.
Denzin, N.K. & Lincoln, Y.S. (1994). *Handbook of qualitative research*. Thousand Oaks, CA: Sage.
Patton, M.Q. (2002). *Qualitative research and evaluation methods*. Thousand Oaks, CA: Sage.

Chapter 4 Surveys and other quantitative approaches

Baruch, Y. & Holtom, B.C. (2008). Survey response rate levels and trends in organizational research, *Human Relations*, 61, 8: 1139–1160.
Hayes, R.J. & Bennett, S. (1999). Simple sample size calculation for cluster-randomized trials, *International Journal of Epidemiology*, 28, 2: 319–326.
Kadam, P. & Bhalerao, S. (2010). Sample size calculation, *International Journal of Ayurveda Research*, 1, 1: 55.

Chapter 5 Research methods

Creswell, J.W. & Poth, C.N. (2017). *Qualitative inquiry and research design: Choosing among five approaches*. Thousand Oaks, CA: Sage.
Miles, M.B., Huberman, A.M. & Saldana, J. (2013). *Qualitative data analysis*. Thousand Oaks, CA: Sage.

Chapter 6 The single case

Merriam, S.B. (1998). *Qualitative research and case study applications in education: Revised and expanded from 'case study research in education'*. San Francisco, CA: Jossey-Bass Publishers.
Yin, R.K. (2013). *Case study research: Design and methods*. Thousand Oaks, CA: Sage.

Chapter 7 Research tools

Mulhall, A. (2003). In the field: Notes on observation in qualitative research, *Journal of Advanced Nursing*, 41, 3: 306–313.
Rodgers, B.L. & Cowles, K.V. (1993). The qualitative research audit trail: A complex collection of documentation, *Research in Nursing & Health*, 16, 3: 219–226.

Chapter 8 Engaging with the literature

Jones, M.L. (2004). Application of systematic review methods to qualitative research: Practical issues, *Journal of Advanced Nursing*, 48, 3: 271–278.
Littell, J.H., Corcoran, J. & Pillai, V. (2008). *Systematic reviews and meta-analysis*. Oxford, UK: Oxford University Press.
Popay, J., Rogers, A. & Williams, G. (1998). Rationale and standards for the systematic review of qualitative literature in health services research, *Qualitative Health Research*, 8, 3: 341–351.

Chapter 9 Qualitative data analysis

Miles, M.B., Huberman, A.M. & Saldana, J. (2013). *Qualitative data analysis*. Thousand Oaks, CA: Sage.
Thomas, D.R. (2006). A general inductive approach for analyzing qualitative evaluation data, *American Journal of Evaluation*, 27, 2: 237–246.

Chapter 10 Evaluating qualitative research

Curtin, M. & Fossey, E. (2007). Appraising the trustworthiness of qualitative studies: Guidelines for occupational therapists, *Australian Occupational Therapy Journal*, 54, 2: 88–94.
Holloway, I. (1997). *Basic concepts for qualitative research*. Chichester, UK: Wiley-Blackwell.
Lietz, C.A., Langer, C.L. & Furman, R. (2006). Establishing trustworthiness in qualitative research in social work implications from a study regarding spirituality, *Qualitative Social Work*, 5, 4: 441–458.
Lincoln, Y.S. & Guba, E.G. (1985). *Naturalistic inquiry*. Thousand Oaks, CA: Sage.
Loh, J. (2013). Inquiry into issues of trustworthiness and quality in narrative studies: A perspective, *The Qualitative Report*, 18, 33: 1.
Morrow, S.L. (2005). Quality and trustworthiness in qualitative research in counseling psychology, *Journal of Counseling Psychology*, 52, 2: 250.
Wall, S. (2006). An autoethnography on learning about autoethnography, *International Journal of Qualitative Methods*, 5, 2: 146–160.

Chapter 11 Writing for publication

Hartley, J. (2008). *Academic writing and publishing: A practical handbook*. Abingdon, UK: Routledge.
Heppner, P.P. & Heppner, M.J. (2004). *Writing and publishing your thesis, dissertation & research: A guide for students in the helping professions* (4th ed). Pacific Grove, CA: Thomson Brooks/Cole.

INDEX

abstract ideas 87
abstraction 22, 25, 32
abstracts 88–89
academic developers 2, 12–13
academic development 14, 68
acceptance rates 68
action research (AR) 5, 13, 15–16, 78, 83, 124
agreement levels 104
analysis methods 108
analysis strategy 42, 100
analysis tools 79
applied research 13
approaches 4, 6, 30, 32, 37–42, 44, 56–57, 86, 94–95, 105, 107, 112–113, 122; analytical 40; critical 13, 127; deductive 105; narrative 41; non-systematic 94; objective 39; phenomenological 39; philosophical 38; pragmatic 31, 50; qualitative 40, 53, 56; reductionist 40; structured 96; systematic 96, 108; tripartite 88
approximation 116
audit trail 115
auditability 9, 113–115; internal 115
auto-ethnography 40
automated user online trails 99

behavioural sciences 112
bell curve 53

case research 70, 75
case studies 7, 69–70, 73–74; educational 69; empirical 123

cases 8, 37, 39, 42, 46, 50, 57, 60, 62, 69–71, 74–78, 124, 127; single 42, 68–70
categories 7, 28, 47, 52, 103, 105–108, 112–113; conceptual 28; empirical 28
causality 51
clinical research 52
clusters 48–49, 101; naturally-occurring 49
Cochrane Reviews 89
coders 104; independent 103
codes 100–106, 108; categorizing 106; emerging 101; generating initial 105
coding 8, 72, 98–105, 107–108, 113; axial 102–103; open 102–103; systematic, 103
coding deployment 99
coding process 108
coding scheme 98–99, 101–102, 104–107
coding strategies 108
coding structure 104
Cohen's kappa coefficient 104
comparative analysis 39
comparative research 107
comparison, systematic 103
complex methodological problems 76
complex social problems 112
compliance 130
computer 65, 79–80, 98
computer-mediated 59
concept formation 87, 94
conceptual ideas 2, 20, 95
conceptualize 87, 100
conclusions: analytical 72; preliminary 59; valid, 52

conditional conclusions 8
consistency 104, 113; internal 118
constant comparison 103
constructionism 22
constructions 40; discursive 105
content analysis 105; directed 105; summative 105
content analysis techniques 105
context 5–6, 8, 11–13, 19–20, 22, 41–42, 57, 59–60, 64–65, 69–70, 79, 84–85, 88, 95–96, 112; historical 90; particular 3, 99, 117; unique 95
control 35, 51–52
convenience sampling 48
conversations 11, 58, 65, 72, 82, 95; methodological 35
covariation 51
credibility 9, 113–114, 116; soliciting 96
criteria: exclusion 88–89, 91; predetermined 107; quantitative 111
critical theory 25
critics of reliability and validity 112
Cronbach's Alpha 118
cultural filters 63
cultural phenomena 1
culture 31, 39–40, 130

data: analyzing 41; central repository of 7, 78; contextual 80; empirical 20, 67; nominal 54; ordinal 54; primary 75; quantitative 61–62, 70–71; secondary 100; source of, 4–5 23, 56, 65–67, 79, 83, 116
data analysis 37, 59, 105, 115–116; deductive 107; latent 107; manifest 107; systematic 114, 116
data analysis process 99
data analysis strategy 42
data collection 7, 32, 34, 37, 40–41, 56, 60, 67, 69, 72, 79, 94, 99, 116; employed empirical 5; methods for 78, 117; transparent 114–115
data interpretations 116
data modelling 46
data validation 99
data verification 114, 116
databases 34, 79, 89; online 89
dataset 57, 103, 105–107
deductive method 105
deliberative spaces 7, 78, 83
dependable outcomes 114–115
depth 6, 16, 24, 41, 46, 62, 94; methodological 30; theoretical 117
description 8, 16, 39, 53, 73, 88–91, 100, 114, 116–117; general 40;
process-oriented 40; thematic 39; thick 4, 38
design 6, 9, 17, 25, 34, 37, 46–47, 54, 60, 68, 122–123; experimental 6, 51
deviations, standard 53
Deweyian pragmatist 31
Dewey's proposition 72
dichotomous 62
digital repositories 34, 80
digital technologies 65
dimensions 9, 15, 35, 52, 83, 88, 113–114; main 113; positive 90; qualitative 61, 111
disciplines 1–3, 5, 7–8, 12–13, 16–18, 36, 68–69, 71, 74, 78–79, 82–83, 112, 118, 129–130
discourses 9, 100, 112–113, 118
discovery 5, 11, 15–17, 40, 58, 71, 122; blue-skies science 123
discovery research 122
distribution 45, 47, 53
double-barrelled questions 63
double negatives 63

education 1–18, 20–21, 31–33, 37, 41–44, 51–53, 57–58, 67–70, 73, 78–79, 84–86, 122–124, 127–128, 130
education analysis 105
education methodologies 69, 130–131
educational research 17, 42, 50
educational theory 74
effect size 50
effectiveness 41, 52
emergent ideas 40, 57
empirical research 4, 6, 16–17, 21, 35, 37, 42; qualitative 23
empiricism 24–25
engagement 1, 24, 30, 33, 71, 85, 87; critical, 8, 90
enhanced rigour 114
epistemic access 2, 6, 21, 32–33, 35–36, 129
epistemological positions 19–21, 24, 31, 34, 36
epistemology 5–6, 19–36, 44, 62; interpretative 38; quantitative 117
error 14, 28, 122; random 47; systematic 47
essence 21, 23, 35, 38, 72
evaluation 116, 118
evaluation methods 77
evidence 9, 24, 27, 30, 38, 46, 55, 71–73, 75, 90, 96, 115, 125–126
experimentation 52–53
experiments 51–52, 55, 65; educational 52; natural 52; scientific 51–52; true 52–53
explanatory power 64, 111

exploration 60, 66, 105; systematic 129
exploratory 39, 98
external auditability 115

factors 4, 39, 50–51; confounding 53
fallacies 96
field experiments 52
field notes 84
findings 47, 72, 74, 91, 95, 112–113, 115–117, 126; contextualizing, 100
framework 5, 8, 87, 98, 111, 113, 129
framing 20, 87–88, 91
Friedman test 54

gap 17, 87, 96, 123, 126
gap statements 96, 123
generalizations 47, 50, 70–71, 105
Grix's interpretation 23
Grix's model 23
grounded theory 6, 37, 39–40, 102
groups 1, 3, 12–13, 38, 52, 54, 61, 82, 94–95; control, 52; distinct, 12; experimental, 52
groups designs 53

hermeneutics 31
heuristics 22, 42
hypothesis 45, 47, 51, 53, 55, 60, 75

ICF (interview context framework) 59
in-depth interviews 46
independent samples 54
inductive approaches 105, 107
inquiry 4–6, 9, 11, 15, 17–18, 21, 31, 69–72, 75, 80, 82, 84, 115, 122; empirical 69; interdisciplinary 1; naturalistic 40; non-systematic 82
instrument: standard 61; validated 62
intercoder reliability 99
intercoder reliability estimates, 104
internal validity, 116
interrupted time-series designs 53
interview sample size 46
interview transcripts 8, 83, 98, 100–102
interviewer-respondent interaction 81
interviews 7, 35, 40–41, 46, 49–50, 56–61, 67, 81–83, 93, 100, 116
IPR (interpersonal process recall) 7, 56, 65–67

judgements 70, 86, 117; subjective 113, 127; suspended 72
justification 85, 96, 123

key argument, 41
key concepts 105

key variables 87
keyword searches 95
knowledge 1–3, 15–18, 20–25, 29–36, 44, 51–52, 61, 68–70, 72–73, 75, 85, 94–96, 107–108, 123–124, 131; case-based 70; conceptual 108; explicit 22; factual 51; historical 96; implicit 22; powerful 87; practical 15; tacit 60
knowledge accumulation 70
knowledge claims 29, 36
knowledge construction 30, 127

labels 4, 12, 105
laboratory 51–52, 79–80
learning analytics 65
learning research methodology 2
legitimate knowledge 3
Likert response scale 62
Likert responses 62
literature 6, 8, 85–97, 100, 102, 108, 113, 127
literature review 8, 72, 81, 85–86, 90, 96–97
lived experience 39, 94
loglinear analysis 54

McNemar test 54
manifests 20, 107
manipulation 55, 65
Mann-Whitney 54
matching strategy 52
materials: qualitative 99; relevant 88; screening 88; selecting 88
mathematical axioms 22
mathematicians 12
meaning making 30
measure: objective 112; quantitative 112
measurement scale 6, 45
measurement theory 62
member checking 116
memos 40, 116
methodological concepts 2
methodological exposition 34
methodological knowledge 2
methodologists 18, 26, 33, 112; qualitative, 20
methodology 1, 7, 18, 24, 26, 29, 31, 33–34, 71, 73, 122, 129, 131; mixed quantitative/qualitative 72; qualitative 3, 111–113; quantitative 111, 117
mixed methods research 3–4, 7, 9, 29, 33–35, 46, 56, 65, 116, 122
mixed methods research design 25
mixed methods research paradigms 21
mixed methods traditions 26

model 8, 18, 73, 86–88, 90, 102; paradigmatic 26
multi-way contigency tables 54
multidisciplinary 17, 127
multistage 48

narrative inquiry 6, 37, 40, 111
natural bias 24
naturalistic settings 51, 64
nominal scales 45
non-parametric models 53
non-probability samples 48
numerical approximations 112
numerical methods 3

objective reality 25
objectivity 22, 29
observational methods 40, 56, 63–64
observational research 67
observations 8, 16, 28, 40, 50, 53, 55, 63–64, 74, 81, 107–108, 127; classroom 67; direct 64
one-way ANOVA 54
ontological access 33
ontological assumptions 23
ontology 6, 19–23, 26–28, 30–31, 33–34; interpretative 98, 112
ontology and epistemology 5–6, 19–36
open interview 58, 81
operationalize 87
ordinal scales 45–46

paired samples 54
paradigms 7, 18, 24–26, 30, 68, 70–71, 112, 116; alternative 24; interpretative 112; qualitative 70; scientific quantitative 29; single 25
parametric statistical models 53
participant consent 64
participant observation 64; direct 65
participants 33, 38–39, 41, 47–50, 52, 56–57, 59–61, 64, 66, 81, 93, 107, 112–113, 115–116, 118; pre-categorizes 107
patterns 15, 99, 102, 105–107, 125
Pearson correlation 54
peer reviewers 18, 30
personal biases 115
perspective 26, 73, 90, 116; epistemological 36; ontological 23; pragmatist 71; professional development, 3; theoretical 117
phenomenological reduction 39
phenomenology 6, 37–40

phenomenon 38–41, 45–46, 53, 57, 60, 63, 65, 98, 100, 102–103, 105, 107, 115, 117; central 38, 116; complex 46, 112; controversial 60; educational 45, 50, 61; observable 45
philosophy 31, 38, 95
plausible alternative explanations 51
population 4, 45–50, 53, 55, 64
population characteristics 45, 49
population of interest 47–49
population statistics 45
positivism 25–27
positivist 11; hegemonic 84
positivist paradigms 118
pragmatism 26–27
pre-and post-test 53
pre-coding data processing 106
precision 112, 124
preliminary data analysis 99
preliminary empirical verification 118
preliminary themes 108
principles 16, 39, 44, 51, 53, 61–62, 65, 104, 131; critical 75; general 24–25; generative 33; hermeneutic 83; verification 116
probability sampling 48–49
probability sampling techniques 47
probability statistics 46
problem formulation 117
problem identification 15
process, 14–16, 22, 24, 29, 31, 56–57, 70–71, 74, 81, 83, 86–90, 98–102, 104–107, 115–116, 129; collective 70; creative 33, 83; critical 24, 71; experiential 71; meaning-making 99; reciprocal 74; systematic 86, 90, 113; validation 80
professional identity 84
professional practice 15, 41, 69
professional researchers 12
proposition 123
protocol 61, 66, 82; clear engagement 61; semi-structured interview 61
purposeful research 29
purposive sampling 48

qualitative data 79, 81, 99–100, 106
qualitative data analysis 8, 98–108
qualitative methods 7, 71, 129
qualitative research methods 11, 118
quality 1–2, 4, 7–9, 13–14, 21–24, 27, 34, 59, 71–75, 83–84, 112–113, 117–20, 123–126, 129–131
quality case research 73

quantitative approaches 6, 37, 42, 44–53, 55, 67, 98, 105, 112
quantitative methods 4, 40, 44, 50, 111, 116
quasi-experimental designs 52
questionnaire design 64
questionnaire layout 63
questionnaire methods 46
quota sampling 48

random sample 49
random sampling 49; stratified 49
randomization 49, 52, 55
randomized controlled trials (RCT) 52
range 2–3, 17, 24, 28, 30, 42, 59–60, 96
rank 45, 62, 126
ratio scales 46
realities: multiple 114, 117
reasoning 23, 67, 71, 105; deductive 102–103, 105; inductive 105; recall 66–67; stimulated 65
recorder 66, 79
recruiting participants 47
referencing tools 81
reflective practice (RP) 15–16, 124
reflexive ideas 25
reflexive self-awareness 29
reflexive statement 115
reflexivity 25, 115
regression analysis 54
relationships 14, 24, 27, 38, 44, 51, 54, 87, 90, 98, 100–103, 113; causal 29, 51; cause-and-effect 51; direct 23; linear 23; presumed cause-effect 51
reliability 62, 70, 111–112, 117–118; intercoder 103–104, 115
replicability 55, 111
representation 41, 81, 98; schematic 90; thematic 107; visual 47
research, repeated 127
research analysis 99
research design 2, 4, 32, 42, 52, 99, 117, 122
research experiments 51
research gap 96
research inquiry 15
research journey 131
research methodologists 30, 35
research methodology 2, 5, 11, 13, 17–18, 42, 94
research methods educators 19
research ontology 34
research paradigms 24–26, 113; interpretative 100; qualitative 122
research phenomenon 40
research philosophy 5, 20–21, 28–30, 33–34

research problem 51, 98–99, 106
research subjects 29, 35, 52
research theory 5
research tools 7, 78–84
research topic 85, 88, 123
research traditions 40
researcher experience 114–115
researcher identity 84
researcher questions 51
respondents 40, 50, 57–58, 63–64, 73, 81, 83, 100, 118
response rate 50, 63, 93
rigour 4, 9, 22, 27, 82, 84, 104, 111–113
rule-based knowledge, contrasting 70

sample 4, 45–50, 62, 73, 108, 125
sample analysis 45
sample size and response rate 50
sample size calculation 50
sample statistics 45
sample transcript 102
sampling 47, 49; cluster, 49; multistage 49; people-in-the-street 48
sampling error 50; small 50
sampling frame 47
sampling procedures 49
sampling strategy 37, 47, 61
sampling techniques 47–49
sampling theory 47
saturation 60, 86, 107; executive 86
scales 45–46, 118
scatter plots 47
science methodology 28
science researcher 80
science subjects 52; quantitative 17
search strategy 88
semantics 24, 101; epistemological 31
semi-structured interview 58
sensors 65, 98
snowball 48
snowball sampling 49
social phenomenon 4
social reality 112
social research 44
social sciences 3, 7, 15, 22, 33, 78, 80, 112
sources 9, 21, 23, 32–33, 51, 90, 94, 104, 116, 122; empirical 5; multiple 46, 71; quantitative 75; secondary 78
Spearman test/Chi Square 54
standardized instrument 62
statistical analysis 44–45, 47, 53
statistical confidence 50
statistical decisions 6, 53
statistical packages 79

140 Index

statistics 47, 53, 62, 104; descriptive 45, 47; inferential 45; subject 1–2, 4–6, 8, 12–14, 17–18, 29–33, 37–38, 41, 54, 74, 85–86, 95, 108, 123–127, 129–131
subject knowledge 85, 130
subjects design 54
summaries 5, 42, 45, 47, 89–91, 94; descriptive 89; representative 46; visual 8, 98
summary statistics 47
super-complex problems 7
survey approaches 6, 45–46
survey design 63
survey instruments 55, 67, 93, 118
surveys 6, 40, 44–53, 55, 63, 67, 93, 116
systematic inquiry 3, 82, 124–125

TACT 9, 113, 118
TACT framework 9, 111–114, 117–118
teaching 1–2, 5, 8–9, 11–16, 52, 57–58, 69–70, 78, 82, 94, 129–130; high quality 14; research informs 82; research-led 58
teaching research methods 9, 11, 23, 96
techniques 4, 22, 48–49, 51, 53, 57, 66, 98, 100, 107; analytical 72; constant comparison 103; interviewing 59; unstructured 59
technology 14, 79, 98
temporal precedence 51
test 45, 53–54, 62, 72, 123; non-parametric 53; parametric 53
textualization 39
thematic analysis 105–108; latent 107
thematic pattern 106
themes 8, 90, 100–102, 104–106, 108, 118, 126; categorizing 113; coded 104; emergent 41; overlapping 113
theoretical framework 105
theoretical position 105
theoretical underpinning 118
theory formation 2, 123
theory integration 17
threshold 104
tools 8, 22, 78–80, 84, 86, 89–91, 94; analytic 108; digital 79, 81

traditions 3–5, 67; qualitative 26–27, 98; quantitative 3, 26–27, 98
transcript corpus 102
transferability 9, 111, 113–114, 117–118
transparency 112, 118
treatment group 52
trials 14, 28, 57, 122; clinical 3; randomized control 53; randomized controlled 52
triangulation 46, 65, 67, 114, 116
tripartite 89
tripartite model 8, 90–91, 94, 96
trustworthiness 9, 113–115, 118
two-way contingency tables 54

undergraduate courses 58
understanding ontology 19
understanding variables 45
undertaking data collection 42
units 49, 101–102, 116
unstated assumptions 76
unstructured forms 57
utility 9, 14, 25, 35, 41, 69, 74, 91, 96; enhancing research 113

validation 62, 90
validity 26, 28, 104, 111–112, 118; external, 117
value judgement 128
value position 16
values 3–5, 11, 15–16, 20–24, 26, 29, 32–34, 38, 57, 84, 96, 104, 112, 118
variables 44–45, 50–52, 54; confounding 51; dependent 51–52; independent, 47; missing 51
variances 53–54
variations 39, 112
verification 41, 116
visualization 99

western democratic ideas 16
Wilcoxon test 54
within-study analysis 90–92
worthwhile contribution 131
worthwhile gap 85
WS-repeated measures 54